EXCLUSIVELY YOURS

By the same author

A History of Perfume

A History of Fashion

The Collector's Book of 20th Century Fashion

Secrets of the Couturiers

A Woman by Design

EXCLUSIVELY YOURS

YOURS

Fashion knits from the world's top designers

Frances Kennett

Prentice Hall Press · New York

Published in 1986 by Prentice Hall Press
A Division of Simon & Schuster, Inc.
Gulf + Western Building
One Gulf + Western Plaza
New York, NY 10023

PRENTICE HALL PRESS is a trademark of
Simon & Schuster, Inc.

This book was designed and produced by
The Rainbird Publishing Group Limited
27 Wrights Lane
London W8 5TZ

Library of Congress Cataloging-in-Publication Data

Kennett, Frances.
  Exclusively yours.

  1. Sweaters.   2. Knitting—Patterns.   I. Title.
TT825.K446   1986   746.9′2   86-5903
ISBN 0-13-293812-X

Manufactured in Italy

10 9 8 7 6 5 4 3 2 1

First Prentice Hall Press Edition

CONTENTS

◆ INTRODUCTION ◆

A luxurious designer knit is perhaps beyond the reach of many of us. We asked the best designers in the world to make their own choice from their work for you to knit yourself. All these designs are exclusively yours.

Enthusiasm for hand-knitting has never been greater. There are more beautiful yarns available now than ever before. This book offers the missing ingredient – high quality design ideas to match your interest in the craft.

Knits are high fashion for all ages – which puts the hand-knitter at a tremendous advantage. It really is possible to make a mohair sweater in a week for less than half the price of the same style off the peg. The higher up the scale of craftsmanship, the greater the saving, not to mention the increase in pleasure that comes from making a beautiful thing.

There is nothing in this book that is above the talents of an average knitter. Some patterns may take a little time, but none require special skill or expertise. So many craft books and magazines promise the reader too much – I sincerely hope that this book will prove the exception, in that it is full of achievable original ideas.

Knitting designers are at work worldwide, and it is interesting to see how different nationalities approach the subject. Several of the American designers offer the very best of high style in fashion – like the immaculate two-piece from Calvin Klein, or the elegant colours of Perry Ellis. Adrienne Vittadini brings Italian glamour to her knits, and has a magical ability with pattern and colouring. Carol Horn's sporty styles are truly American, while Joan Vass's styles correspond more to the European tradition for the eccentric, craft-oriented look.

British designers were in the forefront of the movement towards the use of fine, natural materials in fashion, from the 1960s on, and are responsible for our continuing admiration for quality and craftsmanship in our clothes. This taste is becoming more refined, not as earthy and homespun as it was years ago. Knitted clothes are no longer big baggy shapes in lovely yarns; now they are neatly shaped, and the surface decoration is carefully planned and balanced. The work of Bill Gibb, Sandy Black, and Sasha Kagan has received critical acclaim worldwide – a large part of their work is never seen in the UK but sells to America, Japan, Italy, and France instead.

In Europe, the story is different again. Women in France, Italy, and Germany know the techniques of knitting much better than we do, and they can 'read' a pattern, altering a neckline or a sleeve to suit their own preferences. Younger knitters in Britain and America should also try to develop more confidence in their ability, and not follow instructions slavishly every time. This is especially true of colourings. There is a temptation to knit a design exactly as it is photographed, and hardly ever to stop to think whether 'that blue' is the best shade for each individual. French knitters would never do that, but then they have a longer family tradition for knitting, whereas we have what Sandy Black calls 'a lost generation', and young girls turning to knitting now are more or less self-taught. For encouragement, look at the Vicky Mora, Beatrice Hympendahl, or La Squadra designs – very European, neat and elegant. They would all look quite stunning in other colours, or with different surface decorations to suit your own tastes.

The patterns in this book have been chosen because of the originality and brilliance of their designers. In a few instances (like the Joan Vass models) the examples are true originals which cannot, and are not intended to be duplicated. The wools are hand-mixed for each of her hats, for example. But the ideas, and the techniques are so clever and easy to copy that they are sure to excite your creative energies. In every case, yarns are recommended but need not be exclusively used. Alternative ways to use the same pattern are also suggested, to give you yet more original knitting projects. The technical section at the end of the book will also help you to make knits that really are, with the help of the world's best designers, exclusively yours.

Frances Kennett

◆ CONVERSIONS & ABBREVIATIONS ◆

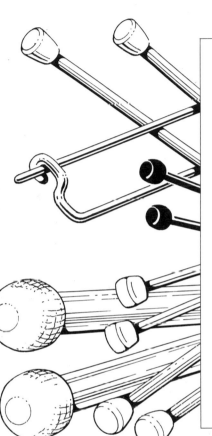
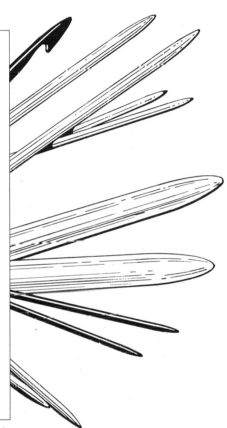

Knitting needles conversion chart

English	US	Continental
13	0	2¼
12	1	2¾
11	2	3
10	3	3¼
9	4	3¾
8	5	4
7	6	4½
6	7	5
5	8	5½
4	9	6
3	10	6½
2	10½	7
1	11	7½
00	13	8½
000	15	9

Abbreviations

approx approximately
beg begin(ning)
ch chain(s)
cm centimetre(s)
cont continu(e) (ing)
dc double crochet (UK) = single crochet (US)
dec decreas(e) (ing)
foll follow(s) (ing)
g gramme(s)
g st garter stitch
in inches
inc increas(e) (ing)
K knit
m metre(s)
mm millimetre(s)
P purl
patt(s) pattern(s)
psso pass slip stitch(es) over

rem remain(s) (ing)
rep repeat(ing)
RS right side
sc single crochet (UK) = double crochet (US)
sl slip
st st stocking stitch (UK) = stockinette st (US)
st(s) stitch(es)
tbl through back of loop(s)
tog together
tr treble (UK) = double crochet (US)
WS wrong side

*repeat instructions following or between *
[ ] repeat directions inside square brackets

Note Figures inside round brackets in instructions refer to larger sizes. When there is only one set of figures, it applies to all sizes.

Perry Ellis

Perry Ellis started as a sportswear buyer until he decided that he could make more interesting clothes of his own. In 1974 he began designing for Seventh Avenue companies to gain experience but by 1978 he was ready to launch his own label, backed by Manhattan Industries. In 1979 he won both the Neiman Marcus Award and the Coty American Fashion Critics' 'Winnie'. Other Coty Awards were awarded to him in subsequent years. Until his recent untimely death in May 1986, he was undoubtedly one of the leaders of American fashion.

A Southerner, with a great appreciation of womanly good dressing, he once said, 'I don't make fashion, I make clothes', and it is true still that his designs have a timelessness and beauty that makes their owners want to keep on wearing them, above fashion. Perry Ellis was also renowned for the quality of cut in his work, believing that clothes could be both modern and classic. He had a subtle, European taste in colouring and proportion, using brilliant jewel-colours in silks, suedes, and richly textured wools for his hand-knits. The design featured here is based on the motifs in Chinese porcelains, demonstrating his genius for using a difficult design resource and translating it into an original style.

◆ DRAGON CARDIGAN ◆

Perry Ellis's white cotton cardigan is inspired by the ornate motifs found on Chinese porcelains.

This design requires patience and close attention to the chart, for the colours are very subtle. Make yourself a chart guide by sticking small lengths of each yarn colour on to a card and writing the chart symbols alongside each one. When using stranding colours as fine as these the yarns need only be *crossed* together; do not make bumps by twisting them too many times (see pages 117-18).

DMC Cotton Perlé No 3 is available internationally (see page 123).

Twilley's *Stalite No 3* can also be used for the white.

MATERIALS

13(14) 50g/1¾oz balls of *DMC Cotton Perlé No 3* in main colour, M (White)
15×15m/20yd *DMC Cotton Perlé No 3* skeins in first contrasting colour B (Dark Navy)
12 skeins each of three contrasting colours, A, C and D (Mid Blue, Very Dark Turquoise, and Bright Blue)
4 skeins each of four contrasting colours, E, F, G and H (Turquoise, Pale Turquoise, Very Pale Turquoise and Very Pale Blue)
1 pair each of 3¾mm/US size 1 and 3¼mm/US size 4 knitting needles
2¾mm/US size 1 circular knitting needle
1 large-eyed darning needle
Four small buttons

SIZE

To fit 86(91)cm/34(36)in bust. See diagram for finished measurements.

TENSION/GAUGE

28 sts and 40 rows to 10cm/4in over st st on 3¾mm/US size 4 needles.

ABBREVIATIONS

See page 11.

Note Use a separate length of yarn for each section and twist yarns together on WS of every row to avoid a hole. Read odd numbered rows K from right to left and even numbered rows P from left to right. For instructions on stranding and Swiss darning see pages 117 and 118-19.

LEFT FRONT

With smaller needles and A, cast on 69(73)sts.
1st row (RS) K1, [P1, K1] to end.
2nd row P1, [K1, P1] to end.
Change to M; then cont in rib for 6 rows more. AT THE SAME TIME, dec 1 st at each end of every other row 4 times [for mitred edge]. 61(65)sts.
Change to larger needles and cont working from chart as foll:
1st-4th rows With M, work in st st.
5th row K41(45)M, K1 B, K19 M.
6th row P20 M, P1 B, P40(44)M.
7th row K39(43)M, K1 B, K21 M.
8th row P22 M, P1 B, P38(42)M.
9th row K36(40)M, K3 B, K22 M.
10th row P24 M, P2 B, P35(39)M.
11th row K34(38)M, K2 B, K25 M.
12th row P26 M, P3 B, P12 M, P2 B, P18(22)M.
These 12 rows set patt.
Cont working from chart until 30th row has been completed.
Front now measures 10cm/4in from beg.

Shape top of side slit

Working extra sts into patt; cast on 4 sts at beg of next row. 65(69)sts.
Cont working from chart until 120th row has been completed.

Shape neckline

121st row (RS) Patt from chart to last 3 sts, K2tog, K1.
Cont dec in this manner on every foll 6th row, 12 times more; then every foll 8th row, 4 times.
AT THE SAME TIME, when 184th row of chart has been completed:

Shape armhole

185th row Cast/bind off 8 sts, patt to end.
Cont shaping neckline as given, until 40(44)sts rem.
When 280th row of chart has been completed, cast/bind off *loosely*.

RIGHT FRONT

Work as for left front reversing all shapings, until 31st row of chart has been completed.

Shape top of side slit

Working extra sts into patt, cast on 4 sts at beg of next row; 65(69)sts;
AT SAME TIME, begin head of dragon thus:
32nd row P35(39)M, P2 A, P28 M.
This row sets patt.
Cont working from chart, shaping neckline at beg of 121st row instead of end and shaping armhole after 185th row of chart has been completed.
Cont to match left front until 280th row has been completed.
Cast/bind off rem 40(44)sts *loosely*.

BACK

With smaller needles and A, cast on 136(144)sts.

1st row (RS) [K1, P1] to end.
2nd row As 1st row.
Change to M and work 6 more rows in rib.
AT THE SAME TIME, dec 1 st at each end of every other row 4 times [for mitred edges]. 128(136)sts.
Change to larger needles and cont working in st st until 30th row above rib has been completed.

Shape top of side slits

Cast on 4 sts at beg of next 2 rows. 136(144)sts.
Cont in st st until 154th row above rib has been completed.
Begin dragon's tail working from chart for left front:
155th row K51(55)M, K1 B, K84(88)M.
Cont working tail from chart until 180th row above welt has been completed.
Begin dragon's head using chart for right front:
181st row Patt until 46(50)sts rem, K2 A, K44(48)sts M.
Cont working in patt, keeping tail and head correct as shown, until 280th row above rib has been completed.
Cast/bind off *loosely*.
Mark both sides of centre 40 sts with a coloured thread for neck.

SLEEVES

With smaller needles and A, cast on 59(59)sts and work in single rib as given for left front rib for 2 rows.
Change to M and work 5 more rows in rib.
Inc row (WS) P to end; inc 7 sts evenly across row. 66(66)sts.
Change to larger needles and work from chart as foll:
1st row (RS) K2 B, K1 H, K1 E, K1 B, K2 D, K1 B, K1 F, K2 B, K3 E, K1 B, K2 D, K4 A, K1 B, K1 F, K1 B, K3 E, K1 B, K2 D, K8 A, K2 D, K1 B, K2 E, K1 B, K2 F, K1 B, K3 A, K3 D, K1 B, K2 E, K1 B, K2 F, K1 B, K2 D, K4 B. 66(66)sts.
This row sets patt. Cont working from chart.

Shape sides

Working extra sts as made in st st in M; inc 1 st at beg and end of 3rd row and every foll 4th row, 39 times more. 146(146)sts.
Cont working in st st on these sts, until sleeve measures 54cm/21in from cast on edge, ending with a WS row.
Cast/bind off *loosely* knitwise.

FRONT AND NECK BANDS

Using circular needle and M, with RS facing, pick up and K 90 sts up right front, 120 sts up right front neck, 40 sts across back neck, 120 sts down left side of front neck and 90 sts down left side of front. 460 sts.
Work 3 rows in K1, P1 rib as given for back, beg and ending with a WS row.
Inc 1 st at beg and end of first and every foll 2nd row, 3 times more for mitred edge.
Buttonhole row (RS) Rib 18, yon, K2tog, [rib 20, yon, K2tog] 3 times, rib to end.
Work 2 more rows in rib. Change to A and work 2 more rows.
Cast/bind off *loosely* in rib.

Side slits

With smaller needles and M and RS of work facing, pick up 20 sts left front side slit.
Work 5 rows in K1, P1 rib as given for back welt.
Change to A and work 2 more rows.
Inc 1 st at lower edge of band on 1st row and every 2nd row 3 times more, for mitred edge.
Work bands for 3 rem slits in the same manner, always inc at lower edge for mitre.

FINISHING

Fasten off all ends neatly on WS of work. Swiss darn sts shown on chart that have not been worked in knitting. Fasten off all ends.
Sew mitred edges of slits neatly

tog. Sew slit bands carefully to cast-on sts of body.
Sew sleeves evenly between coloured markers, with centre of sleeves at shoulder seams. Sew side and sleeve seams tog, sewing ribs edge to edge. Press garment lightly as instructed on yarn label, avoiding ribbing. Press all seams on WS of work. Sew on buttons opposite buttonholes.

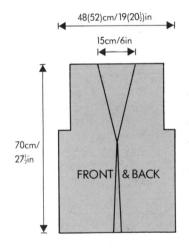

FRONT & BACK

48(52)cm/19(20½)in
15cm/6in
70cm/27½in

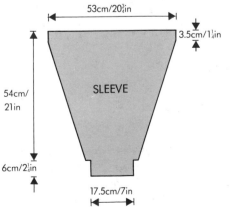

SLEEVE

53cm/20¾in
3.5cm/1¼in
54cm/21in
6cm/2½in
17.5cm/7in

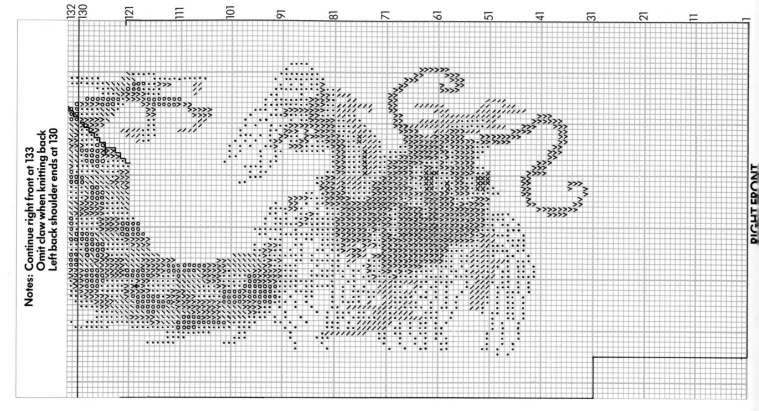

Notes: Continue right front at 133
Omit claw when knitting back
Left back shoulder ends at 130

RIGHT FRONT

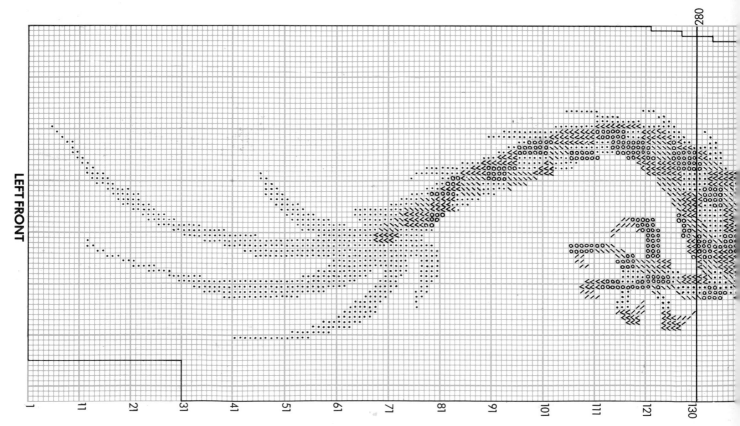

LEFT FRONT

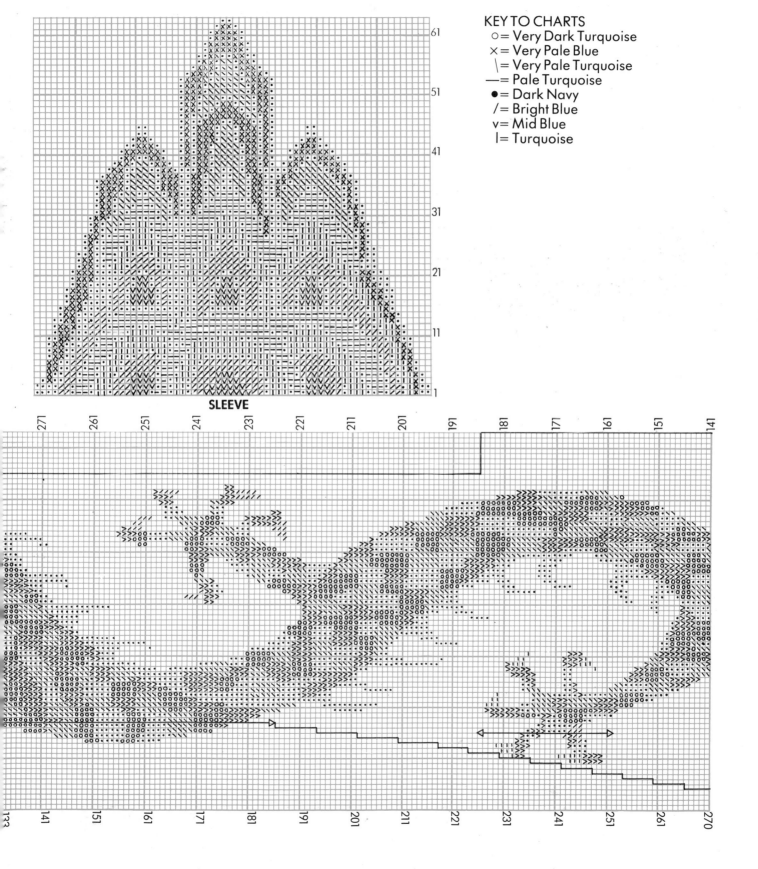

KEY TO CHARTS
- o = Very Dark Turquoise
- x = Very Pale Blue
- \ = Very Pale Turquoise
- — = Pale Turquoise
- ● = Dark Navy
- / = Bright Blue
- v = Mid Blue
- l = Turquoise

SLEEVE

Sandy Black

Sandy Black's distinctive approach to knitting fashion justifies her international reputation. Sandy started designing knits during her student days; her subject was mathematics and she works with a high degree of technical skill and variety in her designs. Some are colourful, some geometric, some textured, nearly all simple shapes. Sandy likes to develop several different themes simultaneously in her collections. 'With knitting, even more than other crafts like weaving, you've never finished with an idea', she says.

Since 1975 Sandy Black has been based in workrooms in London's dockland area, Rotherhithe, and has produced hundreds of exclusive garments, ninety per cent of which sell for export. Sandy has also had great success with her own designs and exclusive yarns in the hand-knit kit market. Knitters send her letters full of enthusiasm for their results. With designers like Sandy to inspire them, hand-knitters can count on the greatest pleasure and satisfaction in their efforts.

• Grid Cardigan •

Sandy Black's cardigan design has impeccable detailing in the positioning of the stripes and the use of various button colours (she admits to a great fondness for buttons!). Other combinations she recommends that work well are white and black with spots of violet and jade; grey and violet with spots of black and yellow; blue and yellow with spots in jade and black. Yellow and orange, or pink, with a black grid and spots in violet, pink or jade, also looks very striking. Refer to the note for *Matisse* on page 22 for further information on the yarn type.

MATERIALS

25×25g/¾oz balls of Sandy Black 100% *Cotton Fizz* in main colour A (Blue)
5 balls in contrasting colour B (Pink)
1 ball each of two contrasting colours, C and D (Yellow and Black)
10 buttons in assorted colours
1 pair each of 3¾mm/US size 5 and 3mm/US size 2 knitting needles
Two stitch holders
1 darning needle

SIZE

To fit 86-97cm/34-38in bust. See diagram for finished measurements.

TENSION/GAUGE

24 sts and 33 rows to 10cm/4in *over grid* patt on 3¾mm/US size 5 knitting needles. Measure the square, width and length, inside the grid lines: 8cm/3¼in square.

Note Use a separate length of yarn for each section and cross yarns together on every row to avoid a hole. It is essential to check tension/gauge carefully before commencing the garment and use the needle sizes which give *you* the correct tension. This may not be the size quoted in the standard tension above, as individual knitters vary.

ABBREVIATIONS

mb – Make bobble: work in B to position of bobble, with C or D, K into front, back, front, back and front of next st (5 loops). Turn and K5, turn and P5, pass 2nd, 3rd, 4th and 5th sts over first st. Place rem stitch in C/D on to left hand needle and K in B. If bobble is on a P row, push bobble through to RS of work. Alternate bobble colours along a row to form diagonal lines overall.

BACK

Using smaller needles and A, cast on 120 sts and work in K2, P2 rib until rib measures 2.5cm/1in. Change to larger needles and B, beg grid patt as foll:
(Best results are obtained by using a separate ball of yarn for each vertical stripe of A and B. On the back there will be 11 balls of yarn used across a row.)
1st row KB.
2nd row PB.
3rd row KB.
4th row P2B, mb, [P22B, mb] 5 times, P2B.
5th row KB.
6th row P4B, [P20A, P3B] 5 times, P1B.
7th row K4B, [K20A, K3B] 5 times, K1B.
Rep rows 6, 7, 12 more times.
32nd row PB.
33rd row KB.
34th row PB.

35th row K2B, mb, [K22B, mb] 5 times, K2B.
36th row PB.
37th row K4B [K20A, K3B] 5 times, K1B.
38th row P4B [P20A, P3B] 5 times, P1B.
Rep rows 37 and 38 12 more times.
These 62 rows form patt repeat. Cont in patt as set until row 106 is complete, and back measures approximately 35cm/13¾in from beg.

Shape armholes

Keeping in patt, cast/bind off 4 sts at beg of next 2 rows; cast/bind off 3 sts at beg of next 4 rows; dec one st at beg of next 8 rows. 92 sts. Work without shaping until row 168 is complete (44th patt row) and back measures approximately 53cm/21in from beg.

Shape shoulders

Cast/bind off 8 sts at beg of next 8 rows. Leave 28 sts rem on holder for neckband.

LEFT FRONT

Pocket linings (make 2)

Using larger needles and A, cast on 26 sts. In st st work 14cm/5½in and leave sts on holder.
Using smaller needles and A, cast on 60 sts. Work in K2, P2 rib for 2.5cm/1in. Change to larger needles and set out grid patt as foll:
1st row KB.
2nd row PB.
3rd row KB*.
4th row P11B, mb, P22B, mb, P25B.
5th row KB.
6th row P10A, P3B, P20A, P3B, P24A.
Cont in grid patt until row 44 is complete.

Divide for pocket

Keeping in patt, K25A, slip next 26 sts on to stitch holder, with RS facing K 26 sts from pocket lining, patt to end. Cont in grid patt until row 106 is complete or until left front matches back to armhole ending with a WS row.

Shape armhole

Cast/bind off 4 sts at beg of next row. Work one row. Cast/bind off 3 sts at beg of next and foll alternate row. Work one row. Cast/bind off one st at beg of next row and foll 3 alternate rows. 46 sts. Cont without shaping until row 149 is complete (25th patt row) or left front measures 48cm/19in, ending with a RS row.

Shape neck

Cast/bind off 6 sts at beg of next row. Work one row. Dec one st at beg of next row and foll 7 alternate rows. 32 sts. Work without shaping until row 170 is complete or left front measures 54cm/21¼in from beg, ending with a WS row.

Shape shoulder

Cast/bind off 8 sts at beg of next row and foll 3 alternate rows.

RIGHT FRONT

Work as for left front to *.
4th row P25B, mb, P22B, mb, P11B
5th row KB.
6th row P24A, P3B, P20A, P3B, P10A.
Cont in grid patt until row 44 is complete.

Divide for pocket

K10A, slip next 26 sts on to st holder, with RS facing K26 sts from pocket lining, patt to end. Cont in grid patt until right front matches back to armhole shaping, ending with a RS row.

Shape armhole

Cast/bind off 4 sts at beg of next row. Work one row. Cast/bind off 3 sts at beg of next and foll alternate row. Work one row. Dec one st at beg of next row and foll 3 alternate rows. 46 sts. Cont without shaping in patt until right front matches left front to neck, ending with a WS row.

Shape neck

Cast/bind off 6 sts at beg of next row. Work one row. Dec one st at beg of next row and foll 7 alternate rows. Work without shaping until right front matches back to shoulder ending with a RS row.

Shape shoulder

Cast/bind off 8 sts at beg of next and foll 3 alternate rows.

SLEEVES

Using smaller needles and A, cast on 56 sts. Work in K2, P2 rib until sleeve measures 2.5cm/1in ending with a P row. Inc one st at beg and end of next row. 58 sts. Change to larger needles and B and beg patt as foll:
1st row (RS) KB.
2nd row PB.
3rd row KB.
4th row P17B, mb, P22B, mb, P17B.
5th row KB.
6th row P16A, P3B, P20A, P3B, P16A.
7th row K16A, K3B, K20A, K3B, K16A.
Cont as set in grid patt, spacing horizontal stripes with 26 rows between and keeping 2 vertical lines only, as set, throughout sleeve and at the same time, inc 1 st at each end of next and every foll 5th row to 76 sts. Cont in patt, but inc one st at each end of every foll 8th row to 90 sts. Work without shaping until sleeve measures 43cm/17in.

Shape top

Cast/bind off 4 sts at beg of next 2 rows. Dec one st at each end of every foll 6th row until 74 sts rem. Dec one st at each end of every row until 32 sts rem. Cast/bind off *loosely*.

NECKBAND

Join both shoulder seams. Using smaller needles and A, pick up and K 108 sts evenly from neck edge, RS facing, and work in K2, P2 rib until neckband measures 5cm/2in. Cast/bind off *loosely* in rib.

POCKET EDGING (both alike)

Place 26 sts from pocket edge back on to smaller needle and using A, work 2.5cm/1in in K2, P2 rib. (If preferred keep continuity of grid lines at beg and end of pocket edging by working 3 sts at each end in B.) Cast/bind off *loosely* in rib.

LEFT FRONT BAND

With smaller needles and A, RS facing, pick up and K 116 sts evenly along front edge, including half neckband, and work in K2, P2 rib until band measures 2.5cm/1in. Cast/bind off *loosely* in rib.

RIGHT FRONT BAND

Work as for left band, but make 10 buttonholes in centre as foll:
1st row Rib 3, [rib 10, cast/bind off 2 sts] to last 3 sts, rib 3.
2nd row Work in K2, P2 rib, casting on 2 sts over the 2 sts cast/bound off in previous row all along row. Complete as for left band.

FINISHING

Press pieces lightly as instructed
on yarn label avoiding ribbing.
Darn in all loose ends. Fold collar
in half to inside and sew edges.
Join side and sleeves seams,
matching up grid pattern carefully
on shoulders and side seams. Sew
in sleeves, making two pleats at
head of sleeve. Sew sides of
pocket edgings to fronts and sew
pocket linings to inside. Sew on
buttons.

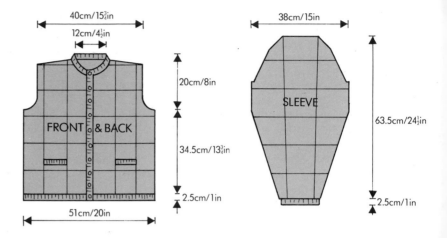

· MATISSE ·

Sandy Black's summer top is
inspired by a collage by Matisse,
and uses the brilliant colours of
Mediterranean summers in an
original design. Her own *Cotton
Fizz* yarn was used for this pattern.
If substituting, try to use a
lightweight, 4-ply cotton with a
similar flaky texture to give an
effect like towelling, rather than a
plain, shiny cotton. Rowan Yarns
make a *Knobbly Cotton* in similar
strong colours which is a suitable
alternative. (See page 115.)

For further information on block
knitting, see page 118.

MATERIALS

18×25g/¾oz balls of Sandy Black
100% *Cotton Fizz*:
5 balls in colour A (Pink)
4 balls in B (Jade)
3 balls in C (Blue)
3 balls in D (Black)
3 balls in E (Yellow)
1 pair each of 4½mm/US size 6
and 2¾mm/US size 1 knitting
needles
6 black buttons
Darning needle

SIZE

To fit 86-97cm/34-38in bust.
See diagram for finished
measurements.

TENSION/GAUGE

20 sts and 28 rows to 10cm/4in
square over st st on 4½mm/US
size 6 needles. It is essential to
check tension carefully before
commencing the garment and to
use the needle sizes which give *you*
the correct tension. This may not be
the size quoted in the standard
tension, as individual knitters vary.

Note Use a separate length of yarn
for each section and cross yarns
together on every row to avoid a
hole. Read odd numbered rows K
from right to left and even
numbered rows P from left to right.

For further information on
adjusting tension, see the section
on Yarn Substitution, on page 118.

ABBREVIATIONS

See page 11.

BACK AND FRONT

With smaller needles and D, cast
on 110 sts and work 3cm/1¼in in
[K1, P1] rib. With larger needles,
working in st st beg chart as foll:
1st row K68A, K42C.
2nd row P42C, P68A.
Repeat these two rows once, then
row one once more.
6th row Using 2 balls B, P42C, P1B,
P66A, P1B.
7th row Using 3 balls B and 2 balls
A, K1B, K12A, K1B, K52A, K2B, K42C.
8th row Using 4 balls B and 3 balls
A, P42C, P3B, P34A, P1B, P16A,
P1B, P11A, P2B.
9th row Using 5 balls B and 4 balls
A, K2B, K10A, K3B, K14A, K3B,
K14A, K1B, K17A, K4B, K42C.
Cont in patt until row 86 of chart is
completed, and front measures
34cm/13½in.

Shape armholes
Cast/bind off 12 sts at beg of next 2
rows. Join in B on next row. Cont in
patt without shaping until chart is
complete, ending with 2 rows of D
as shown, and front measures
57cm/22½in.

Cast/bind off *loosely*, placing markers on 18th and 69th sts for neck: opening measures 25cm/10in

ARM BANDS

Make two bands in B and two in C as foll: using smaller needles, cast on 66 sts and work in [K1, P1] rib until 7.5cm/3in are completed. Cast/bind off *loosely* in rib.

COLLAR

Using A and smaller needles, cast on 152 sts and make one piece as for armband.

FINISHING

Lightly press all pieces excluding ribbing as instructed on yarn label. Carefully darn in loose ends, closing any gaps. Join shoulder seams up to markers. With RS together, pin collar in place, starting and finishing at shoulder seam. Leaving collar open at the side, sew in position from WS, using a flat edge-to-edge seam (see page 116).

For the armbands: with RS tog and using backstitch seams, join cast/ bound off edge of C bands to E armhole edges, and B bands to B armhole edges. Fit each band *squarely* into armhole so corner of armband fits into inner corner of armhole. Overlap 5cm/2in of each armband on to cast/bound off sts at underarm and stitch in place, leaving rem 2.5cm/1in of rib band over to be joined to opposite band at underarm (see diagram).

Join side seams. Sew one button on to each corner of collar as illustrated. Join tog outer corners of armbands by sewing one button front and back at same time.

KEY TO CHART
D = · = Black
E = / = Yellow
A = Pink
B = Jade
C = Blue

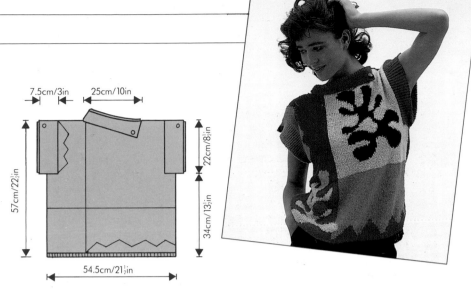

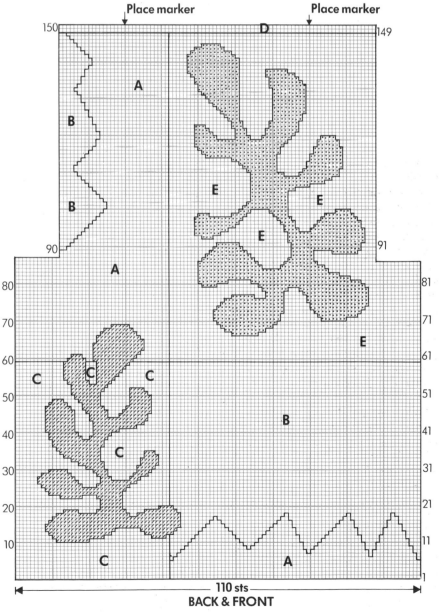

Joan Vass

Joan Vass is a warm, idiosyncratic, multi-talented woman who went into
fashion design ten years ago after a long and interesting career as a
museum curator and art expert (The Museum of Modern Art and
Christie's, New York). She started out making 'One Of a Kind' or 'OOK'
hats, blending scraps of yarn together to produce a colour effect like an
artist's palette. Other knits followed, and now clothes which are high-
style pieces reminiscent of other ages: tunics, robes, frock-coats, in
wonderful fabrics, impeccably stitched.

She lives and works in a glass-roofed loft in New York's Chelsea,
surrounded by jazz records and boxes of beautiful yarns. Her designs
have a name, not a number, to suit the individualistic women who like her
collections. For example, the two-piece here is called the 'DTS' (dog-
tooth stripe) and the beautiful sweater, Baby Iguana. Joan Vass knits are
sophisticated pieces in styling and colouring – she hopes that hand-
knitters will play with the ideas shown here to create their own inimitable
versions, in other colours and other yarns.

·*The DTS Suit*·

Joan Vass uses this apparently simple but carefully conceived design in a variety of styles – for a suit, as here, or for a long tube dress in a plain medium-heavy weight worsted or thicker double-knit yarn. If you want to try other yarns, choose colours that are 'close' to each other, such as cinnamon, orange and pink, for the three shades. If you use a pure wool, strand it or use block knitting technique (see page 118).

MATERIALS

Sweater
200g/7oz in total of Woolgatherers Silk/Mohair/Wool mix *Manchou* in first colour A (Maroon)
100g/3½oz in second colour B (Blue)
150g/5oz in third colour C (Green)

Skirt
100g/3½oz in A
160g/6oz in B
1 pair of 5mm/US size 8 knitting needles
Set of four 4mm/US size 7 double pointed needles
5mm/US size 8 crochet hook
Waist length of elastic

SIZES

To fit 86(91:97)cm/34(36:38)in bust.
See diagram for finished measurements.

TENSION/GAUGE

18 sts and 19 rows to 10cm over stripe patt on 5mm/US size 7 needles.
17 sts and 16 rows to 10cm/4in over check patt on 5mm/US size 7 needles.

Note Strand yarn not in use *loosely* across WS of work to keep fabric elastic. Read odd numbered rows K from right to left and even numbered rows P from left to right.

ABBREVIATIONS

dc – double crochet/US single crochet. Also see page 11.

Pullover

BACK AND FRONT (worked in one piece)

With pair of 5mm/US size 8 needles and B, cast on 88(92:96)sts.
1st row (RS) K 8(10:8)B, [8A, 8B] to last 0(2:0)sts, K 0(2:0)B.
2nd row P 8(10:8)B, [8A, 8B] to last 0(2:0)sts, P 0(2:0)A. **
Rep the last 2 rows until work measures 16cm/6¼in from beg, ending with a P row.
Beg with row 1 and working in st st throughout, cont in patt from chart until work measures 46(48:50)cm/18(18¾:19½)in from beg, ending with a P row.

Shape front neck
Next row Patt 25(27:29), turn and leave rem sts on a spare needle. Dec one st at beg of next and foll 2 alternate rows. 22(24:26)sts. Work one row without shaping. *
Break off yarns and leave these sts for the present.
Return to sts on spare needle; with RS facing, sl first 38 sts on to a holder for neckband, rejoin yarns to neck edge and patt to end. Cont to match first side to *. Thus ending with a K row.

Back neck
Next row Patt to end, cast on 44 sts, then with WS facing, patt across sts which were left. 88(92:96)sts.
Cont without shaping until work measures approximately 84(88:92)cm/33(34½:36¼)in from beg, ending with an 8th row on chart.
Next row (RS) K 8(10:8)A, [8B, 8A] to last 0(2:0)sts, K 0(2:0)A.
Next row P 8(10:8)A, [8B, 8A] to last 0(2:0)sts, P 0(2:0)A.
Rep the last 2 rows until back measures the same as front. Cast/bind off.

SLEEVES

With pair of 5mm/US size 8 needles and B, cast on 50 sts.
1st row (RS) K1A, [8A, 8B] to last st, K1B.
2nd row P 1B, [8B, 8A] to last st, P1A.
Rep the last 2 rows until sleeve measures 16cm/6¼in from beg, ending with a P row and inc one st at each end of last row. 52 sts.
Beg with row 1 and working throughout in st st, cont in patt from chart inc one st at each end of the 5th and every foll 6th row, working inc sts into patt, until there are 60(62:64)sts. Cont without shaping until sleeve measures 42cm/16½in from beg, ending with a P row.
Cast/bind off *loosely*.

NECKBAND

With set of four double pointed needles and RS facing, working throughout in 8 sts A, 8 sts B, pick up and K7 sts evenly down left front neck, K front neck sts from holder, then pick up and K7 sts evenly up right front neck and 44 sts evenly across back neck. 96 sts.
Work 18 rounds in st st keeping colours as set. Cast/bind off *loosely*.

FINISHING

Press pieces according to instructions on yarn label. Sew in sleeves, with centre of sleeve to shoulder seam. Join side and sleeve seams. Fold neckband in half to inside and sew in place. Press seams.
With crochet hook, B and RS facing, work 1 round in dc/sc along lower edge of body and sleeves and fold of neckband (see page 119).

SKIRT

BACK AND FRONT (alike)

Work as given for sweater to **.
Rep the last two rows until back measures 55(58:61)cm/
21½(22¾:24)in from beg, ending with a P row. Break off A.
Work 12 rows st st in B. Cast/bind off *loosely*.
Work front in the same way, reversing colours of stripe patt.

FINISHING

Press pieces according to instructions on yarn label. Join side seams. Fold waistband in half to inside and sew in place, leaving a small opening for elastic. Press seams. Thread elastic through waist and join to form a circle. Join opening. With hook, B and RS facing, work 1 round in dc/sc along lower edge (see page 119).

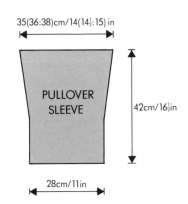

35(36:38)cm/14(14½:15) in

PULLOVER SLEEVE

42cm/16½in

28cm/11in

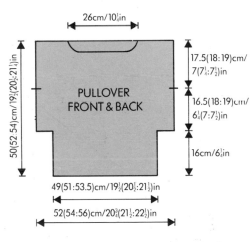

26cm/10¼in

PULLOVER FRONT & BACK

50(52:54)cm/19½(20½:21¼)in

17.5(18:19)cm/
7(7¼:7½)in

16.5(18:19)cm/
6¼(7:7½)in

16cm/6¼in

49(51:53.5)cm/19½(20½:21½)in

52(54:56)cm/20¾(21½:22½)in

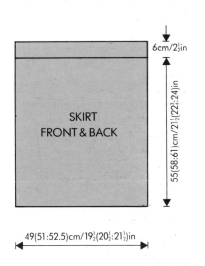

6cm/2½in

SKIRT FRONT & BACK

55(58:61)cm/21½(22½:24)in

49(51:52.5)cm/19½(20½:21½)in

KEY TO CHART
C = □
A = √

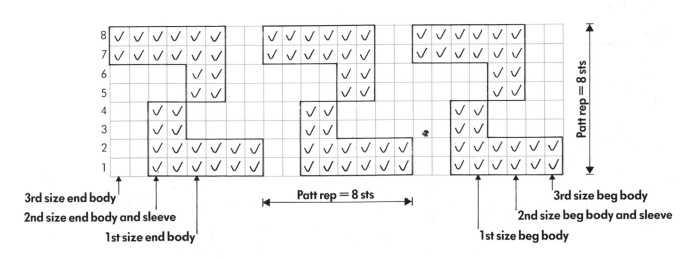

8
7
6
5
4
3
2
1

Patt rep = 8 sts

3rd size end body
2nd size end body and sleeve
1st size end body

Patt rep = 8 sts

3rd size beg body
2nd size beg body and sleeve
1st size beg body

Sasha Kagan

Sasha Kagan studied painting and printmaking at London's Royal
College of Art and sometimes wonders how her career might have
developed if she had actually trained in textiles or knitting: certainly no
more successfully than it has. She was designing theatre costumes in
Oswestry when the chance came to buy a farm in Wales. Working from
Caersws in Cambria, since 1972 she has built up a successful
hand-knit enterprise.
'Sometimes I think I see the world through graph-paper eyes!' she smiles;
a world of endearing motifs, flowers, leaves, kittens, puppies or splashes
of colour in abstract shapes. Clearly she is attracted to textile design by
her taste for original patterning on the surface of quite simple knit shapes.
Nearly 100 per cent of her work sells for export; with a gleam in her eyes
she notes that buyers from all over the world trek to her current
workshop in an early nineteenth-century town house in Llanidloes.
Her loyalty to her skilled team of 150 hand-knitters is matched
by their pride in her design capabilities. That steadiness
derives from the example of her mother, a resourceful,
creative woman who taught Sasha how to knit as a child.
Sasha's own knitting book sold in staggering quantities
worldwide, besides the kits that she markets.
Another book on family designs is on the way, and
will be much appreciated by her four children,
who inspired its contents.

· SQUIGGLE SWEATER ·

Sasha Kagan's *Squiggle Sweater* is worked out in bands of background colour, so that no more than two yarns are being held in the hands for knitting in at any one time. The overall effect looks much more complicated than the actual work involved. You can substitute another 3-ply Botany wool that is available nearer to you, but please note that if you use a synthetic 3 ply, the total amount of wool required will be less, because synthetics weigh less than pure wools.

MATERIALS

6×25g/1oz balls of Rowan *3 Ply Botany* in main colour B (Black)
6×25g/1oz balls in second colour G (Grey)
4 balls in each of 2 contrasting colours A and C, (Pale Green and White)
3 balls in contrasting colour D (Blue)
1 ball in each of 2 contrasting colours E and F, (Rust and Bottle Green)
1 pair each of 2¾mm/US size 2 and 3¾mm/US size 5 knitting needles
Set each of four 2¾mm/US size 2 and 3¼mm/US size 3 double pointed needles.

SIZE

To fit 86-97cm/34-38in bust.
See diagram for finished measurements.

TENSION/GAUGE

28 sts and 28 rows to 10cm/4in over patt on 3¾mm/US size 5 needles.
32 sts and 32 rows to 10cm/4in over patt on 3¼/US size 3 needles.

Note Strand yarn not in use across wrong side of work to keep fabric elastic and weave yarns in only when working across 5 or more sts. Read odd numbered rows K from right to left and even numbered rows P from left to right.

ABBREVIATIONS

M1 – pick up loop lying between sts and work into back of it.
Also see page 11.

BACK

With 2¾mm/US size 2 needles and B, cast on 145 sts.
1st row (RS) K1 tbl, [P1, K1 tbl] to end.
2nd row P1, [K1 tbl,P1] to end.
Rep the last 2 rows until rib measures 8cm/3¼in from beg, ending with a first row.
Inc row Rib 9, M1, [rib 7, M1] 18 times, rib to end. 164 sts.
Change to 3¾mm/US size 5 needles. Beg with a K row and working in st st throughout, cont in patt from chart, working 22 st patt rep across work until all sts are used. Cont in patt as set until back measures 42cm/16½in from beg, ending with a P row.

Shape armholes
Keeping patt correct, cast/bind off 14 sts at beg of next 2 rows. 136 sts. Cont without shaping until armhole measures 29cm/11½in, ending with a P row.

Shape shoulders
Cast/bind off 17 sts at beg of next 2 rows, then 13 sts at beg of next 4 rows. Leave rem 50 sts on a holder for neckband.

FRONT

Work as given for back until armholes measure 19cm/7½in, ending with a P row.

Shape neck
Next row Patt 52, turn and leave rem sts on a spare needle.
Dec one st at neck edge on next 9 rows. 43 sts.
Cont without shaping until armhole measures the same as on back, ending with a P row.

Shape shoulder
Cast/bind off 17 sts at beg of next row, then 13 sts at beg of foll alternate row. Work one row without shaping, then cast/bind off rem sts.
Return to sts on spare needle; with RS facing, sl first 32 sts on to a holder for neckband, rejoin yarns to neck edge and patt to end. Cont to match first side, reversing all shaping.

SLEEVES

With 2¾mm/US size 2 needles and B, cast on 63 sts and work 8cm/3¼in in rib as on back, ending with a 2nd row and inc one st in centre of last row. 64 sts.
Change to 3¾mm/US size 5 needles. Beg with a K row and working in st st throughout, cont in patt from chart, inc one st at each end of the 3rd and every foll alternate row, working inc sts into patt, until there are 162 sts. Cont without shaping until sleeve measures 52cm/20¾in from beg, ending with a P row. Place a marker at each end of last row, then work 14 rows more. Cast/bind off *loosely*.

NECKBAND

Join shoulder seams.
With set of four 2¾mm/US size 2 needles, B and RS facing, pick up and K 34 sts evenly down left front neck, K front neck sts from holder, pick up and K 34 sts evenly up right front neck, then K back neck sts from holder. 150 sts.
Work 12 rounds in K1, P1 twisted rib. Cast/bind off *loosely* in rib.

FINISHING

Press pieces lightly as instructed on yarn label, avoiding ribbings. Sew in sleeves, with rows above markers to cast/bound off sts at underarm. Join side and sleeve seams. Press seams.

HAT

With set of four 2¾mm/US size 2 needles and B, cast on 160 sts and work 12cm/4¾in in rounds of K1, P1 twisted rib, inc 38 sts evenly across last round. 198 sts.

Change to set of four 3¼mm/US size 3 needles. Beg with a K row and working throughout in *rounds* of st st, cont in patt from chart until 46 rows of chart are complete, inc 2 sts evenly across the last row. 200 sts.
Break off colours, cont in B only.

Shape crown
1st round [K8, sl 1-K1-psso] to end.
Work 2 rounds without shaping.
4th round [K7, sl1-K1-psso] to end.
Work 2 rounds without shaping.
7th round [K6, sl 1-K1-psso] to end.
Work 2 rounds without shaping.
Cont as set, dec 20 sts on next and every foll 3rd round until 40 sts rem. Work 2 rounds without shaping.
Next round [K2tog] to end.
Work 2 rounds without shaping.
Rep last 3 rounds twice more. 5 sts.
Break off B, thread through rem sts, draw up tight and fasten off securely.

KEY TO CHART
B = □ = Black
A = / = Pale Green
C = — = White
E = ● = Rust
F = · = Bottle Green
D = \ = Blue
G = × = Grey

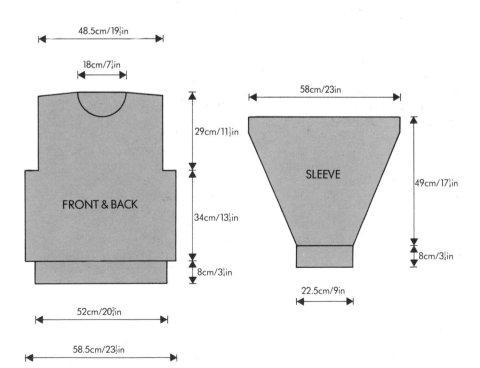

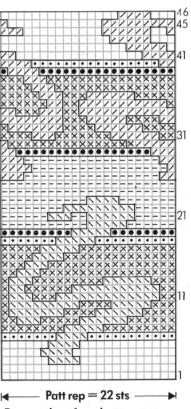

Patt rep = 22 sts
Repeat chart from bottom to top

· CUBE WAISTCOAT ·

Sasha Kagan's *Cube* waistcoat has been carefully designed so that small blocks of certain colours are used, without stranding yarns over wide areas of knitting. She chose Scheepjeswol 4-stranded *Mayflower Cotton* for its bright colours, but other makes of cotton of the same weight could be substituted.

MATERIALS

4×50/1¾oz balls of Scheepjeswol 4-strand *Mayflower Cotton* in main colour W (White)
3 balls in first contrasting colour G (Grey)
1 ball in each of 6 colours (Pale Blue A, Black B, Turquoise T, Dark Blue C, Kingfisher K, and Purple P.)
1 pair each of 2¾mm/US size 2 and 3¼mm/US size 3 knitting needles
5 buttons

SIZE

To fit 81-91cm/32-36in bust. See diagram for finished measurements.

TENSION/GAUGE

32 sts and 32 rows to 10cm over patt on 3¼mm/US size 3 needles.

Note Strand yarn not in use *loosely* across wrong side of work to keep fabric elastic and weave yarns in only when working across 5 or more sts. Read odd numbered rows K from right to left and even numbered rows P from left to right.

ABBREVIATIONS

M1 – pick up loop lying between sts and work into back of it.
Also see page 11.

BACK

With smaller needles and W, cast on 125 sts.
1st row (RS) K1 tbl, [P1, K1 tbl] to end.
2nd row P1, [K1 tbl, P1] to end.
Rep the last 2 rows until rib measures 10cm/4in from beg, ending with a first row.
Inc row Rib 12, M1, [rib 4, M1] 25 times, rib to end. 151 sts.
Change to larger needles. Beg with a K row and working in st st throughout, cont in patt from chart, working 20 st patt rep across work until all sts are used. Cont until back measures 59cm/23¼in from beg, ending with a P row. Cast/bind off.

LEFT FRONT

With smaller needles and W, cast on 56 sts.
1st row (RS) [K1 tbl, P1] to end.
2nd row [K1 tbl, P1] to end.
Rep the last 2 rows until rib measures 10cm/4in from beg, ending with a first row.
Inc row Rib 3, M1, [rib 5, M1] 10 times, rib to end. 67 sts.
Change to larger needles. Beg with a K row and working in st st throughout, cont in patt from chart until left front measures 29cm/11½in from beg, ending with a P row.

Shape front edge
Keeping patt correct, dec one st at front edge on next and every foll 3rd row until 37 sts rem. Cont without shaping until left front measures the same as back to shoulders, ending with a P row. Cast/bind off.

RIGHT FRONT

With smaller needles and W, cast on 56 sts.
1st row (RS) [P1, K1 tbl] to end.
2nd row [P1, K1 tbl] to end.
Cont as given for left front, reversing shaping.

BUTTONHOLE BAND

Join shoulder seams.
With smaller needles, W and RS facing, pick up and K 94 sts evenly up right front to beg of shaping, 98 sts to shoulder seam, then 39 sts to centre back neck. 231 sts.
Beg with a 2nd row, work 4 rows in rib as on back.
Next row Rib 139, [cast/bind off 4, rib 17] 4 times, cast/bind off 4, rib to end.
Next row Rib 139, casting on 4 sts over each 4 cast/bound off. Work 4 more rows. Break off W. Join in P, work one row, then cast/bind off in rib.

BUTTON BAND

With smaller needles, W and RS facing, pick up and K 39 sts evenly across back neck, 98 sts to beg of front shaping, then 94 sts to lower edge. 231 sts.
Beg with a 2nd row, work 10 rows in rib as on back. Break off W. Join in P, work one row, then cast/bind off in rib.

ARMHOLE BORDERS

Place a marker on side edges of back and fronts 24cm/9½in down from shoulders. With smaller needles, W and RS facing, pick up and K 153 sts evenly between markers. Work from *to *on button band.

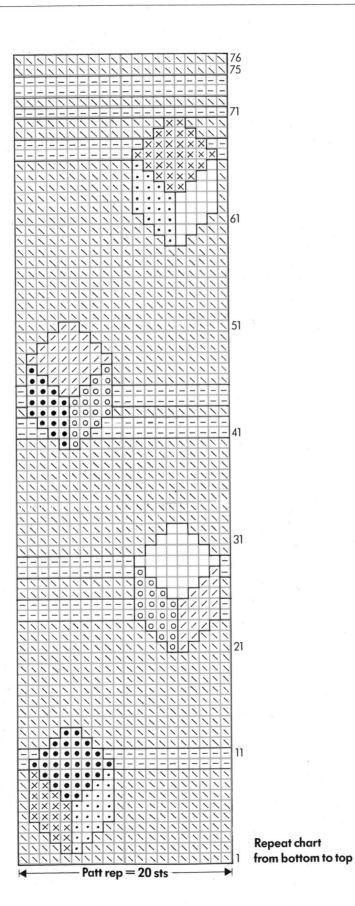

76
75

71

61

51

41

31

21

11

1

Repeat chart from bottom to top

Patt rep = 20 sts

FINISHING

Press pieces lightly as instructed on yarn label, avoiding ribbing. Join side seams and ends of armhole borders. Join ends of front bands at centre back on neck. Press seams. Sew on buttons.

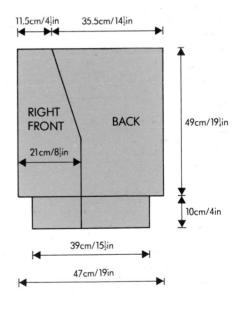

11.5cm/4½in   35.5cm/14½in

RIGHT FRONT   BACK

49cm/19¼in

21cm/8½in

10cm/4in

39cm/15½in

47cm/19in

KEY TO CHART
W = — = White
G = \ = Grey
B = □ = Black
T = / = Turquoise
A = ○ = Pale Blue
C = ● = Dark Blue
K = · = Kingfisher
P = × = Purple

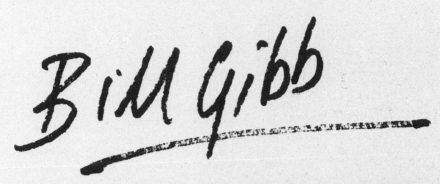

Bill Gibb

Bill Gibb was the designer who turned knitwear into high fashion in the 1960s, rescuing it from its twinset 'war economy' image. He collaborated with Kaffe Fassett to produce intarsia knits, some hand-made, some machined pieces, with pattern motifs as rich as Persian art in their colours and intricacy.

Besides working exclusively as a couturier, specializing in wedding and ball gowns, Bill has relaunched a successful retail collection much acclaimed for its originality.

He likes knitted designs: 'You can magic it up from the yarn itself' and enjoys the pliability in knit shapes. 'Knitted surfaces give you so many elements to play with — pattern, colour, texture and shape. I get more satisfaction when all of it works than I do even from a beautiful ball gown.'

Originally from a large family in Scotland, Bill has never lost an unassuming friendliness. He designed this evening sweater exclusively for this book, to prove that even the most timid knitter could make something very special, using easy-to-find materials. It has all the hallmarks of his best work: an attention to decorative detail, a flattering line, and a clarity of design.

· GLITTER RIB SWEATER ·

Bill Gibb's glamorous evening sweater or 'Sloppy Joe' shape is a perfect design for knitters of moderate skill, and is designed to work in widely available yarns – a medium weight mohair and a glittery yarn for the rib. Pingouin *Mohair 50* and Twilley's *Goldfingering* were used; both yarns are available in many other colours for you to work out your own versions on the theme. Do not be alarmed at the measurements given on the chart – the rib does stretch to fit even generous hips!

MATERIALS

8×50g/1¾oz balls of Pingouin *Mohair 50* in main colour A (Black)
2 balls each of Twilley's *Goldfingering* in three contrast colours, A (Multi) B (Black) and C (Gold)
1 pair each of 3¼mm/US size 3 and 3¾mm/US size 5 knitting needles
Set of four 3¼mm/US size 3 double pointed needles
2 shoulder pads

SIZE

To fit 81-91cm/32-36in bust. See diagram for finished measurements.

TENSION/GAUGE

22 sts and 31 rows to 10cm over patt on 3¾mm/US size 5 knitting needles.

Note Two strands of *Goldfingering* are used tog throughout.

ABBREVIATIONS

T2L – P into back of 2nd st on left hand needle, K first st, then sl both sts off needle tog.
T2R – K into front of 2nd st on left hand needle, P first st, then sl both sts off needle tog.
C2B – K into back of 2nd st on left hand needle, K first st, then sl both sts off needle tog.
C2F – K into front of 2nd st on left hand needle, K first st, then sl both sts off needle tog.
Also see page 11.

BACK

With smaller needles and B, cast on 91 sts.
1st row (WS) P1, [K1, P1] to end.
2nd row K1, [P1, K1] to end.
Rep the last 2 rows 16 times more, *BUT* working throughout in stripes of 1 row C, 3 rows A, 1 row C, 2 rows B, thus ending with 3 rows A. Break off A, B and C.
Change to larger needles and cont in M.
Next row P1, inc in next st, [P3, inc in next st] 22 times, rib to end. 114 sts.
Cont in rib patt as foll:
1st row P4, [K6, P4] to end.
2nd row K4, [P6, K4] to end.
Rep the last 2 rows twice more.
7th row P4, [K2, yarn to front of work between needles, then to back of work over right hand needle to form new loop – called yarn forward or yfwd –, K2tog, K2 P4] to end.
8th row As 2nd row.
9th row P4, [K1, yfwd, K2tog tbl, K2tog, yfwd, K1, P4] to end.
10th row As 2nd row.
11th row P4, [K3, yfwd, K2tog tbl, K1, P4] to end.
12th row As 2nd row.
Rep 1st and 2nd rows 4 times more.

These 20 rows form the rep of patt. Work 100 more rows as set.

Shape raglans
1st row Cast/bind off 6, K1, [T2L, K1, P4, K1, T2R] to last 7 sts, K3, P4.
2nd row Cast/bind off 6 sts, K2, [P1, K6, P1, K2] to end.
**3rd row P2tog, [T2L, P4, T2R, P2] to last 10 sts, T2L, P4, T2R, P2tog.
4th row [K2, P1, K2] to end.
5th row P2tog, [T2L, P2, T2R, P4] to last 8 sts, T2L, P2, T2R, P2tog.
6th row K2, [P1, K2, P1, K6] to last 6 sts, [P1, K2] twice.
7th row P2tog, [T2L, T2R, P2, yarn to back of work over right hand needle, then to front of work between needles – called yarn around needle or yrn –, P2tog, P2] to last 6 sts, T2L, T2R, P2tog.
8th row K2, [P2, K8] to last 4 sts, P2, K2.
9th row P2tog, T2L, [P2, yrn, P2tog, P2tog tbl, yrn, P2, C2B] to last 12 sts, P2, yrn, P2tog, P2tog tbl, yrn, P2, T2R, P2tog.
10th row K2, [P1, K8, P1] to last 2 sts, K2.
11th row P2tog, [T2L, P3, yrn, P2tog, P1, T2R] to last 2 sts, P2tog.
12th row K2, [P1, K6, P1, K2] to end.
Rep rows 3-6 once more.
17th row P2tog, [T2L, T2R, P6] to last 6 sts, T2L, T2R, P2tog.
18th row As 8th row.
19th row P2tog, T2L, [P8, C2F] to last 12 sts, P8, T2R, P2tog.
20th row As 10th row.
21st row P2tog, [T2L, P6, T2R] to last 2 sts, P2tog.
22nd row K2, [P1, K6, P1, K2] to end. **
Rep rows 3-22 until 26 sts rem, ending with a WS row. Cast/bind off.

FRONT

Work as given for back until 34 sts rem.

Shape neck
1st row K2, P1, K8, cast/bind off 12 sts, K8, P1, K2.
Work on last set of sts only:
2nd row P2tog, T2L, P3, yrn, P2tog, P2.
3rd row Cast/bind off 2 sts, K5, P1, K2.
4th row P2tog, T2L, P4.
5th row Cast/bind off 2 sts, K2, P1, K2.
6th row P2tog, T2L, P1.
7th row P2tog, K2.
8th row P2tog, P1.
K2tog and fasten off.
Return to sts which were left; with WS facing, rejoin M to neck edge, P2, P2tog, patt to last 2 sts, P2tog. Cont to match first side, reversing all shaping.

SLEEVES

With smaller needles and B, cast on 49 sts and work 34 rows in striped rib as on back. Break off A, B and C.
Change to larger needles and M.
Next row P3, [inc in next st, P2] 15 times, P1. 64 sts.
Cont in rib patt as on back, inc one st at each end of the 3rd and every foll 5th row, working inc sts into patt until there are 104 sts. Work 2 rows without shaping. Place a marker at each end of last row.
Cont in patt as foll:
1st row P2, [T2L, K1, P4, K1, T2R] to last 2 sts, P2.
2nd row K3, [P1, K6, P1, K2] to last st, K1.
3rd row P3, [T2L, P4, T2R, P2] to last st, P1.
4th row K4, [P1, K4] to end.
5th row P4, [T2L, P2, T2R, P4] to end.
6th row K5, [P1, K2, P1, K6] to last 9 sts, P1, K2, P1, K5.
7th row P5, [T2L, T2R, P2, yrn, P2tog, P2] to last 9 sts, T2L, T2R, P5.
8th row K6, [P2, K8] to last 8 sts, P2, K6.

9th row P6, [C2B, P2, yrn, P2tog, P2tog tbl, yrn, P2] to last 8 sts, C2B, P6.
10th row As 8th row.
11th row P5, [T2R, T2L, P3, yrn, P2tog, P1] to last 9 sts, T2R, T2L, P5.
12th row As 6th row.
13th row P4, [T2R, P2, T2L, P4] to end.
14th row As 4th row.
15th row P3, [T2R, P4, T2L, P2] to last st, P1.
16th row As 2nd row.
17th row P2, [T2R, P6, T2L] to last 2 sts, P2.
18th row K2, [P1, K8, P1] to last 2 sts, K2.
19th row P2, K1, [P8, C2F] to last 11 sts, P8, K1, P2.
20th row As 18th row.
21st row P2tog, [T2L, P6, T2R] to last 2 sts, P2tog.
22nd row K2, [P1, K6, P1, K2] to end.
Rep from ** to ** on back until 46 sts rem, ending with a WS row.
Next row P2tog, T2L, [P2, P2tog, P2tog, P2, C2F] to last 12 sts, P2, P2tog, P2tog, P2, T2R, P2tog.
Cast/bind off.

RAGLAN TRIMS (make 4)

With smaller needles and B, cast on 11 sts and work in striped rib as on back until band is long enough to fit raglan shaping, ending with 3 rows in A. Leave sts on a holder.

NECKBAND

Sew raglan trims to raglan shaping on sleeves and body, with sts on holders to neck edge.
With set of four double-pointed needles, C and RS facing, pick up and K 24 sts evenly across back neck, rib 11 from trim, pick up and K 35 sts evenly across left sleeve, rib 11 from trim, pick up and K 32 sts evenly around front neck, rib 11 from trim, pick up and K 35 sts evenly across right sleeve, rib 11 from trim. 170 sts.
Work 8 rounds in K1, P1 rib, working in stripes of 2 rounds, B, 1

round C, 3 rounds A, 1 round C and 1 round B. Cast/bind off in rib using B.

FINISHING

Press pieces lightly according to instructions on yarn label, omitting ribbing. Join side and sleeve seams. Press seams. Sew in shoulder pads.

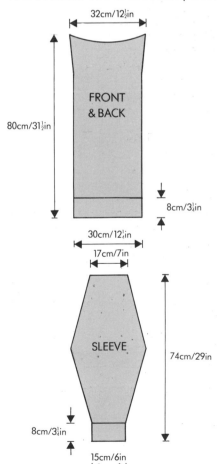

Adrienne Vittadini

Born in Hungary, educated in America, and married to an Italian, Adrienne Vittadini brings a cosmopolitan sophisticated style to her knitwear designing. Her clothes have the glamour and high style associated more with Italian couture than any other. Her own very Monica Vitti-ish looks and unaggressive style are perhaps an influence on her ideas – she likes soft shapes, feminine decorative motifs and flattering, clear colours. Adrienne has technique to match her strong fashion sense. She studied with Louis Féraud in Paris, and worked for major companies like Kimberly Knits before launching on her own in New York in 1975. She is now a leader in the field, and in 1984 won a Coty Award, the fashion world's 'Oscar'.

'Once I tasted the creativity of knitwear I never wanted to go back to wovens. Knits are more of a challenge because one must begin by creating the basic ingredient – the fabric itself. It is so contemporary. Knitted fabric is practical and yet there's a seductive quality too, because it clings to the body.'

· FLOWERS & FERNS ·

These two gorgeous tropical designs are typical of Adrienne Vittadini's talent for pattern and colour. She often has yarns specially dyed to achieve exactly the shades she requires. Fortunately Scheepjeswol *Mayflower Cotton* is available in these subtle shades too, but you could create different effects with other colourways and other stranded cottons (8 ply).

Look at the charts to see how carefully the pattern is varied on each sleeve and over the back.

MATERIALS

(Short-sleeved Sweater)
8 × 50g/1¾oz balls of Scheepjeswol *Mayflower Cotton* in main colour M (Mustard).
2 balls in each of 2 contrasting colours W (White) and P (Purple).
1 ball in each of 4 contrasting colours B (Brown), C (Cerise), G (Green) and R (Red).
1 pair each of 3¾mm/US size 5 and 4mm/US size 6 knitting needles
2 shoulder pads.

SIZE

To fit 86-97cm/34-38in bust.
See diagram for finished measurements.

TENSION/GAUGE

23 sts and 28 rows to 10cm/4in over st st on 4mm/US size 6 needles.

Note Use a separate length of yarn for each section and twist yarns together on every row to avoid a hole. Read odd numbered rows K from right to left and even numbered rows P from left to right.

ABBREVIATIONS

See page 11.

BACK

With smaller needles and M, cast on 113 sts.
1st row RS K1, (P1, K1) to end.
2nd row P1, (K1, P1) to end.
Rep the last 2 rows twice more, inc 7 sts evenly across the last row. 120 sts.
Change to larger needles. **
Beg with a K row, work 56 rows in st st.
Cont in patt as foll:
57th row K 40M, 1W, 1Purple, 1W, 77M.
58th row P 77M, 1W, 1 Purple, 1W, 40M.
This sets position of patt. Beg with row 59 and working throughout in st st, cont in patt from chart until 192 rows in all have been worked from top of rib and chart is complete.

Shape shoulders
Next row Working in colours as set, cast/bind off 42 sts, K to last 42 sts, cast/bind off to end.
Leave rem 36 sts on a holder for neckband.

FRONT

Work as given for back to **
Beg with a K row, row 1 and working throughout in st st, cont in patt from chart, working all decs as shown.

Note When shaping neck; leave centre 16 sts on a holder for neckband, work decs 3 sts in from edge, ie. on left side of neck; RS rows will be "K to last 4 sts, K2tog, K2" and WS rows "P2, P2tog, P to end". On right side of neck; RS rows will be "K2, Sl 1-K1-psso, K to end" and WS rows "P to last 4 sts, P2tog tbl, P2".

SLEEVES

With smaller needles and M, cast on 83 sts and work 6 rows in rib as on back, inc 6 sts evenly across the last row. 89 sts.
Change to larger needles. Beg with a K row, row 1 and working throughout in st st, cont in patt from chart, working all shaping as shown.

NECKBAND

Join right shoulder seam.
With smaller needles, M and RS facing, pick up and K 23 sts evenly down left front neck, K front neck sts from holder inc 3 sts evenly across them, pick up and K 23 sts evenly up right front neck, then K back neck sts from holder inc 4 sts evenly across them. 105 sts.
Beg with a 2nd row, work 6 rows in rib as on back. Cast/bind off *loosely* in rib.

FINISHING

Press pieces lightly as instructed on yarn label, avoiding ribbing. Join left shoulder and neckband seam. Sew in sleeves, with centre of sleeve to shoulder seam. Join side and sleeve seams. Press seams. Sew in shoulder pads.

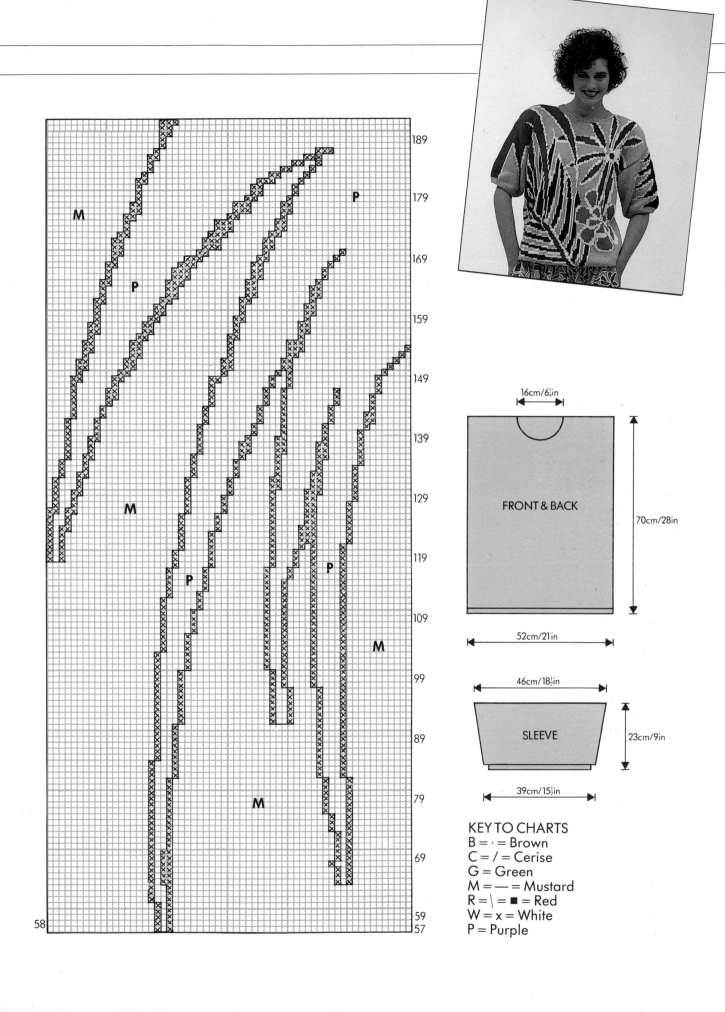

189
179
169
159
149
139
129
119
109
99
89
79
69
59
57

58

M

P

P

M

P

M

P

M

16cm/6¼in

FRONT & BACK

70cm/28in

52cm/21in

46cm/18½in

SLEEVE

23cm/9in

39cm/15½in

KEY TO CHARTS
B = · = Brown
C = / = Cerise
G = Green
M = — = Mustard
R = \ = ■ = Red
W = x = White
P = Purple

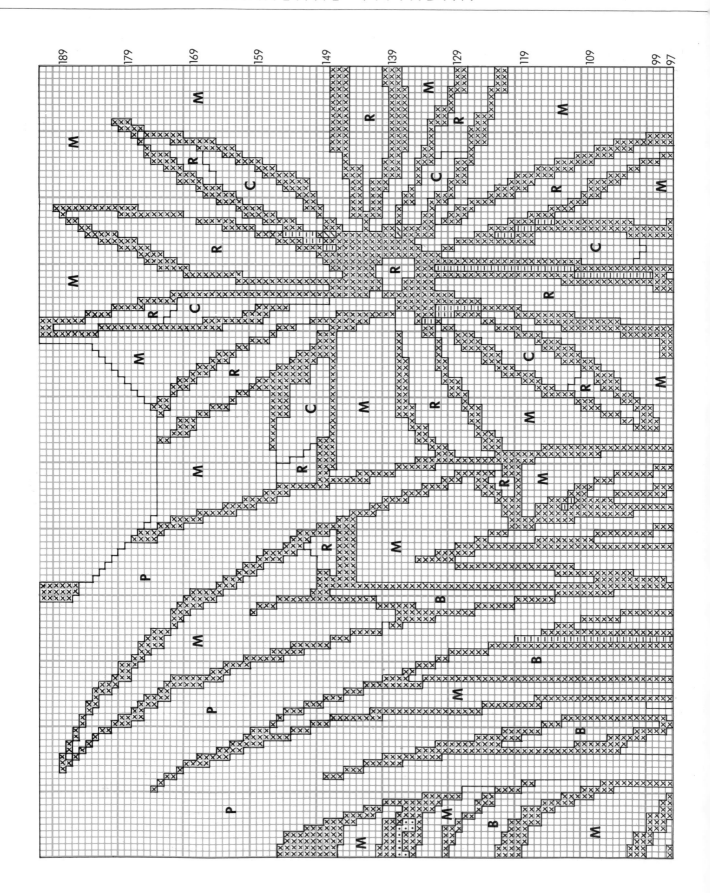

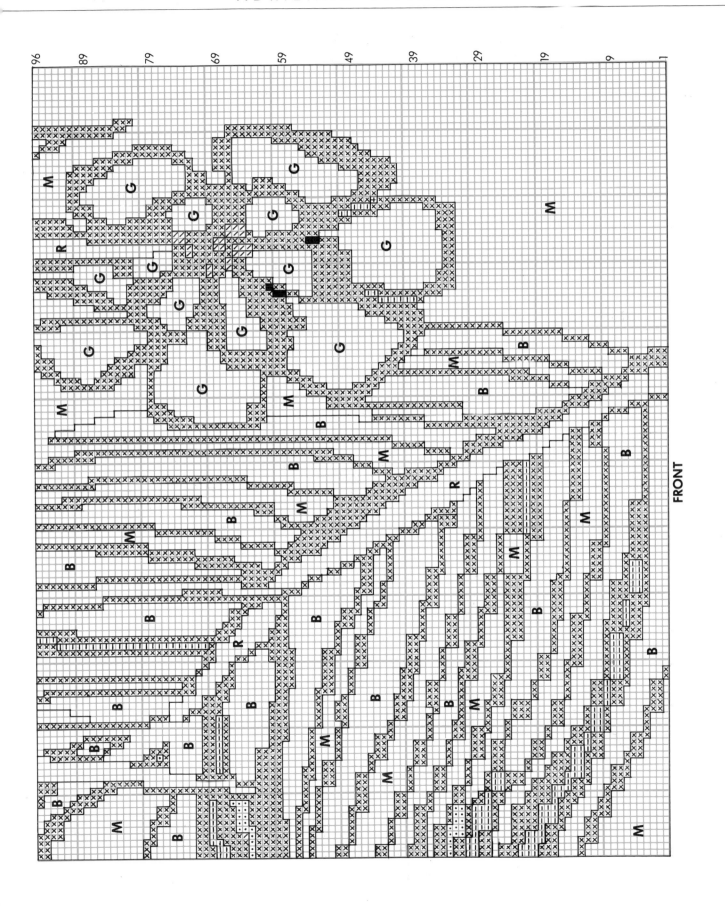

FRONT

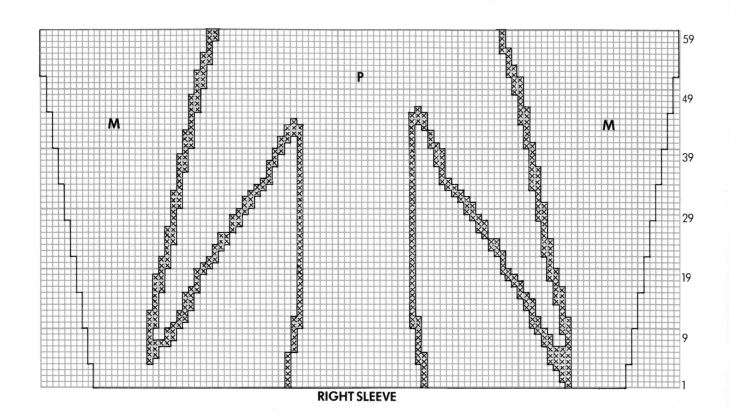

RIGHT SLEEVE

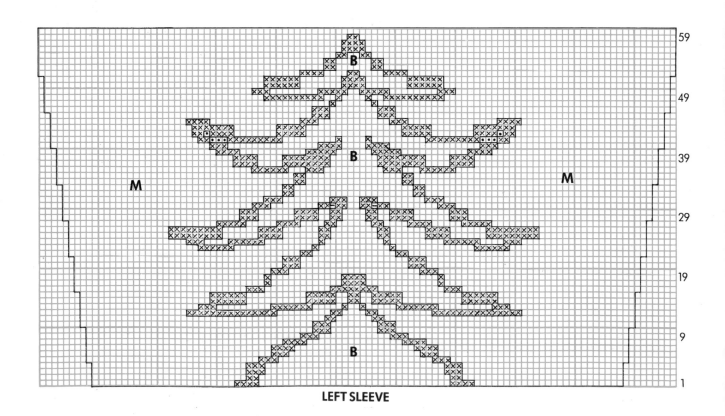

LEFT SLEEVE

·*F*LOWERS & *F*ERNS·

MATERIALS

(Long-sleeved Sweater)
9×50g/1¾oz balls of
Scheepjeswol *Mayflower Cotton*
in main colour G (Green)
2 balls in each of 2 contrasting
colours B (Blue) and M (Mustard)
1 ball in each of 4 contrasting
colours C (Cerise), P (Purple), R
(Red) and W (White)
1 pair each of 3¾mm/US size 5
and 4mm/US size 6 knitting
needles
2 shoulder pads

SIZE

To fit 86-97cm/34-38in bust.
See diagram below.

TENSION/GAUGE

23 sts and 28 rows to 10cm/4in over
st st on 4mm/US size 6 needles.

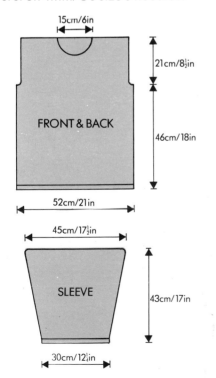

Note Use a separate length of yarn
for each section and twist yarns
together on every row to avoid a
hole. Read odd numbered rows K
from right to left and even
numbered rows P from left to right.

ABBREVIATIONS

See page 11.

BACK

With smaller needles and G, cast
on 119 sts.
1st row (RS) K1, [P1, K1] to end.

2nd row P1, [K1, P1] to end.
Rep the last 2 rows twice more, inc
one st in centre of last row. 120 sts.
Change to larger needles. ******
Beg with a K row, work 101 rows in
st st. Cont in patt as foll:
102nd row P 39G, 1M, 80G.
103rd row K 80G, 1M, 39G.
This sets position of patt. Beg with
row 104 and working throughout
in st st, cont in patt from chart until
122 rows in all have been worked
from top of rib.

Shape armholes
Keeping patt correct as set, cast/

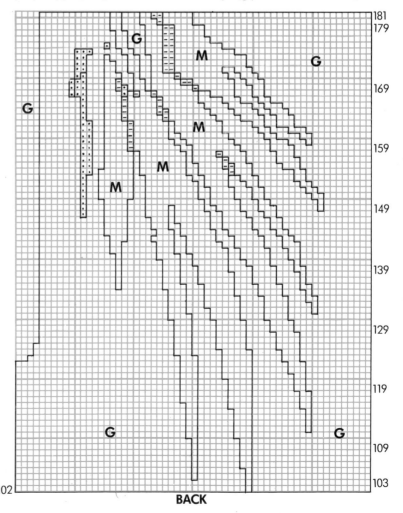

BACK

bind off 2 sts at beg of next 2 rows, then dec one st at each end of next and foll alternate row. 112 sts. Cont without shaping until 181 rows in all have been worked from top of rib and chart is complete.

Shape shoulders
Next row With G, cast/bind off 39 sts, K to last 39 sts, cast/bind off to end.
Leave rem 34 sts on a holder for neckband.

FRONT

Work as given for back to ******.
Beg with a K row, row 1 and working throughout in st st, cont in patt from chart, working all shaping as shown.

Note When shaping neck; leave centre 20 sts on a holder for neckband, work decs 3 sts in from edge, ie. on left side of neck; RS rows will be "K to last 4 sts, K2tog, K2" and WS rows "P2, P2tog, P to end". On right side of neck; RS rows will be "K2, sl1-K1-psso, K to end" and WS rows "P to last 4 sts, P2tog tbl, P2".

SLEEVES

With smaller needles and G, cast on 67 sts. Work 6 rows in rib as back, inc 3 sts evenly across last row. 70 sts. Change to larger needles. Beg with a K row, row 1 and working

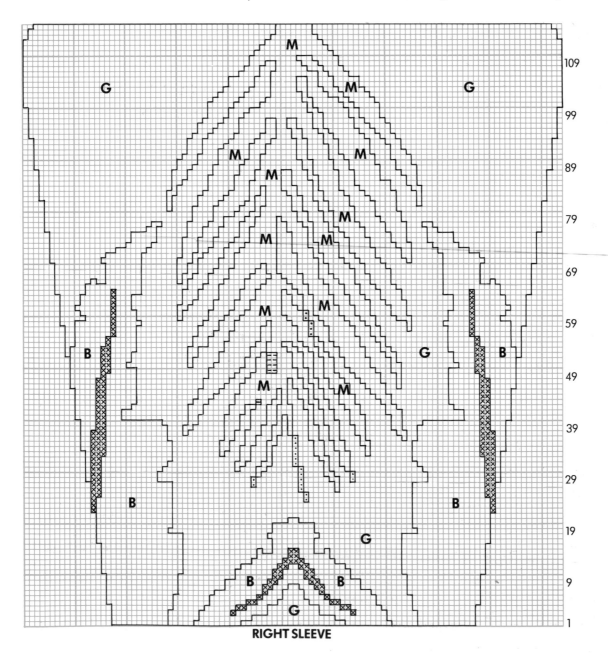

RIGHT SLEEVE

throughout in st st, cont in patt from chart, working shaping as shown.

NECKBAND

Join right shoulder seam.
With smaller needles, G and RS facing, pick up and K 20 sts evenly down left front neck, K front neck sts from holder inc one st in centre of them, pick up and K 20 sts evenly up right front neck, then K back neck sts from holder inc 4 sts

evenly across them. 99 sts.
Beg with a 2nd row, work 6 rows in rib as on back. Cast/bind off *loosely* in rib.

FINISHING

Press pieces lightly as instructed on yarn label, avoiding ribbing. Join left shoulder and neckband seam. Sew in sleeves. Join side and sleeve seams. Press seams. Sew in shoulder pads.

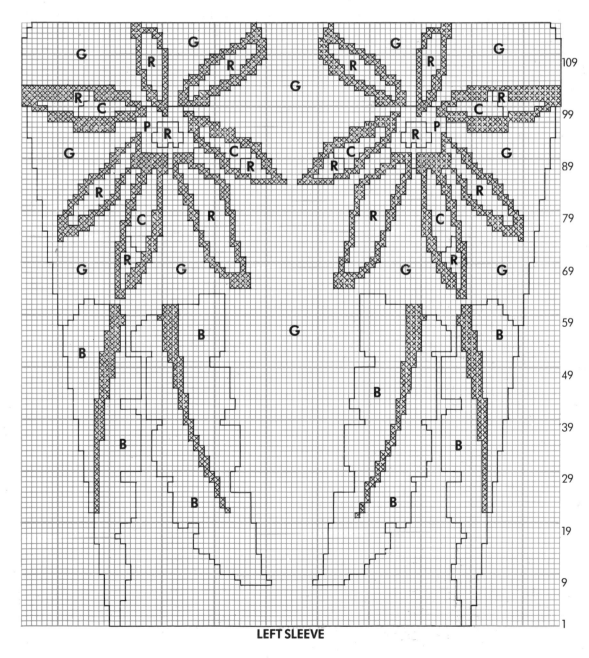

LEFT SLEEVE

KEY TO CHARTS
B = Blue
C = / = Cerise
G = — = Green
M = · = Mustard
P = ● = Purple
R = \ = Red
W = x = White

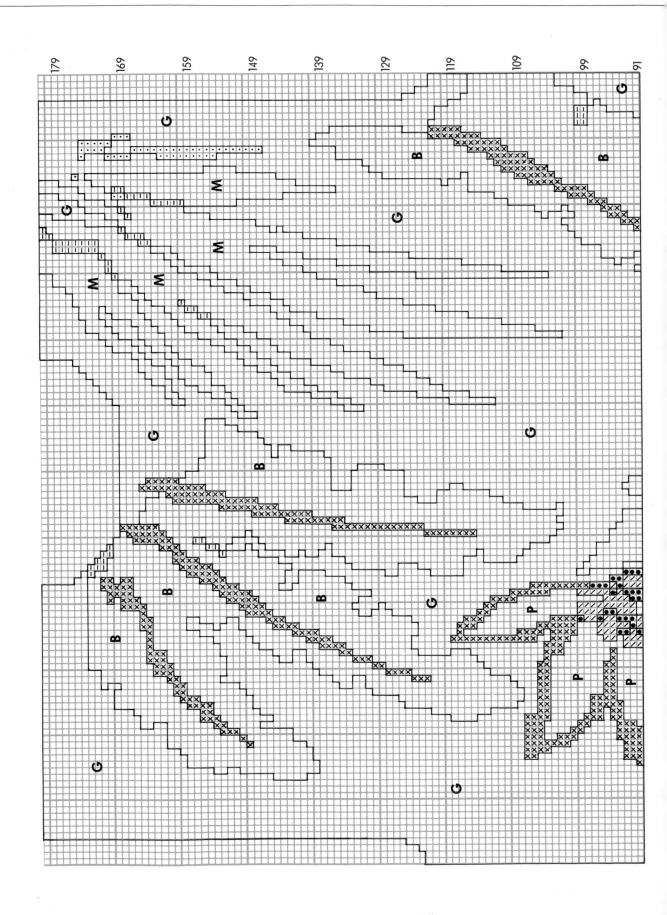

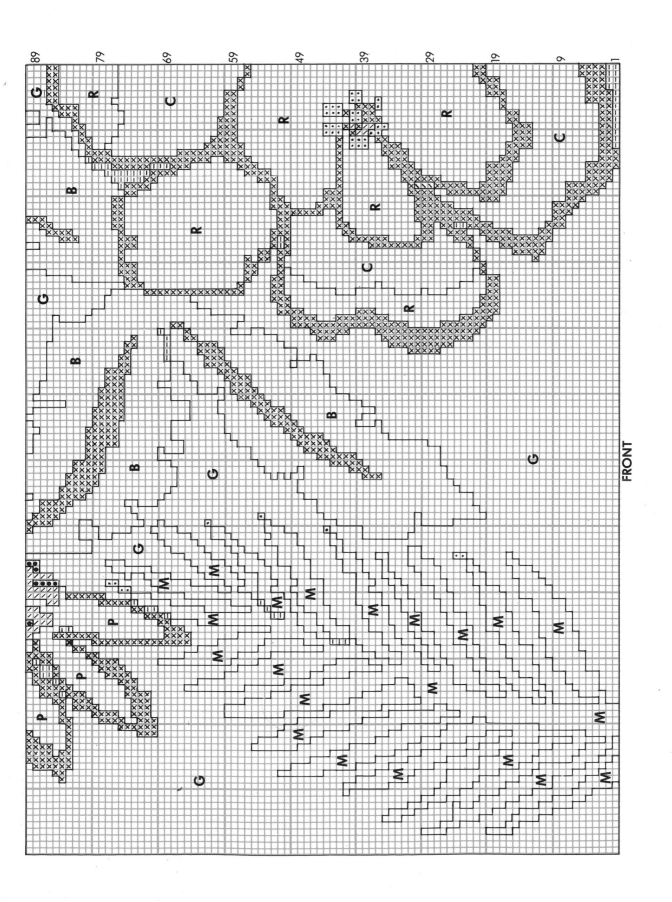

FRONT

• *V*ASARELY •

This dramatic design by Adrienne Vittadini is based on the art of Vasarely, inspired by his strong shapes and bold colours. It is easy to knit with separate balls for the various areas of colour – use two for the two sides of the off-white motif without stranding across the back. Anny Blatt's *Bora Bora* has a 'good red' and an ecru (not a hard white) which are well suited to this design, but there are other shades and other stranded (8 ply) cottons that could be used too. The mini-skirt instructions match both *Vasarely* and *Giraffe Spots*.

MATERIALS

9×50g/1¾oz of balls of Anny Blatt's *Bora Bora Stranded Cotton* in first colour B (Black)
2 balls in second colour E (Ecru)
1 ball in third colour R (Red)
1 pair each of 4mm/US size 6 and 4½mm/US size 7 knitting needles
2 shoulder pads

SIZE

To fit 81(86:91:97)cm
32(34:36:38)in bust.
See diagram for finished measurements.

TENSION/GAUGE

18 sts and 26 rows to 10cm/4in over st st on 4½mm/US size 7 needles.

Note Use a separate length of yarn for each section and twist yarns together on every row to avoid a hole.

ABBREVIATIONS

See page 11.

FRONT

With smaller needles and B, cast on 87(91:95:99)sts.
1st row (RS) K1, [P1, K1] to end.
2nd row P1, [K1, P1] to end.
Rep the last 2 rows once more, inc one st in centre of last row.
88(92:96:100) sts.
Change to larger needles and beg with a K row, work 22 rows in st st.
Cont in patt as foll: ******
1st row K 14(16:18:20)B, 4E, 70(72:74:76)B.
2nd row P 67(69:71:73)B, 9E, 12(14:16:18)B.
This sets position of chart. Beg with row 3 and reading RS rows K from right to left and WS rows P from left to right, cont in patt as set until 134 rows of chart are complete. Work 6 rows in B.

Shape neck
Working throughout in B:
141st row K 34(36:38:40), turn and leave rem sts on a spare needle. Dec one st at neck edge on next 5 rows.
Work one row without shaping. Dec one st at beg of next and every foll alternate row until 26(28:30:32)sts rem. Work 2 rows without shaping. Cast/bind off. Return to sts on spare needle; with RS facing, sl first 20 sts on to a holder for neckband, rejoin B to neck edge and K to end. Cont to match first side, reversing shaping.

BACK

Work as given for front to ******.
1st row K 70(72:74:76)B, 4E, 14(16:18:20)B.
2nd row P 12(14:16:18)B, 9E, 67(69:71:73)B.
This sets position of chart. Beg with row 3 and reading RS rows K from left to right and WS rows P from right to left, thus reversing patt, cont as set until 134 rows of chart are complete. Work 20 rows in B.

Shape shoulders
Cast/bind off 26(28:30:32)sts at beg of next 2 rows. Leave rem 36 sts on a holder for neckband.

SLEEVES

With smaller needles and B, cast on 61(65:69:73)sts and work 4 rows in rib as on back. Change to larger needles and beg with a K row cont in st st, inc one st at each end of the 5th and every foll 4th row until there are 75(79:83:87)sts. Cont without shaping until sleeve measures 14cm/5½in from beg, ending with a P row. Cast/bind off *loosely*.

NECKBAND

Join right shoulder seam.
With smaller needles, B and RS facing, pick up and K 13 sts evenly down left front neck, K front neck sts from holder, pick up and K 12 sts evenly up right front neck, then K back neck sts from holder. 81 sts.
Beg with a 2nd row, work 4 rows in rib as on back.
Cast/bind off *loosely* in rib.

FINISHING

Press pieces lightly as instructed on yarn label avoiding ribbing.
Join left shoulder and neckband seam.
Sew in sleeves, with centre of sleeve to shoulder seam. Join side and sleeve seams.
Press seams.
Sew in shoulder pads.

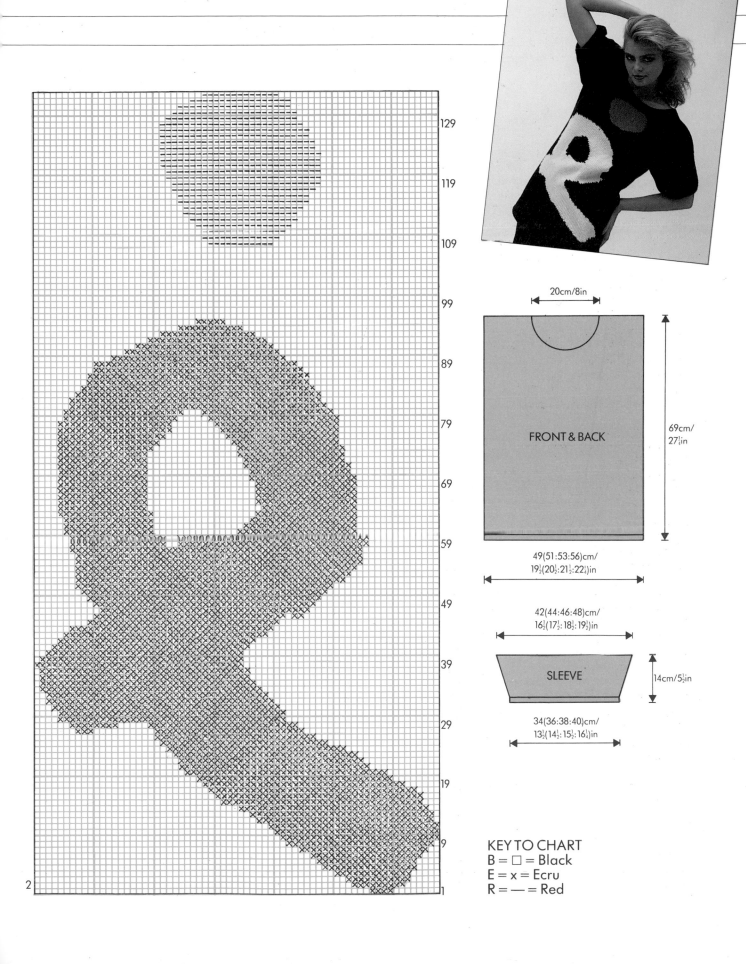

129

119

109

99

89

79

69

59

49

39

29

19

9

2

1

20cm/8in

FRONT & BACK

69cm/
27¼in

49(51:53:56)cm/
19½(20½:21½:22¼)in

42(44:46:48)cm/
16½(17½:18½:19½)in

SLEEVE

14cm/5½in

34(36:38:40)cm/
13½(14½:15½:16¼)in

KEY TO CHART
B = □ = Black
E = x = Ecru
R = — = Red

· GIRAFFE SPOTS ·

The irregular shaping of the black and white motifs brings to mind the beautiful variety in animal hides — like a giraffe. Use separate balls of colour for the white markings. Anny Blatt's *Bora Bora* has a soft, off-white which is suitable for this pattern; other stranded cottons (8 ply) could be used too.

MATERIALS

8×50g/1¾oz balls of Anny Blatt's *Bora Bora Stranded Cotton* in first colour B (Black).
7 balls in second colour E (Ecru)
1 pair each of 3¾mm/US size 5 and 4mm/US size 6 knitting needles
2 shoulder pads

SIZE

To fit 86-97cm/34-38in bust.
See diagram for finished measurements.

TENSION/GAUGE

21 sts and 28 rows to 10cm/4in over st st on 4mm/US size 6 needles.

Note Use a separate length of yarn for each section and twist yarns together on every row to avoid a hole. Read odd numbered rows K from right to left and even numbered rows P from left to right.

ABBREVIATIONS

See page 11.

BACK

With smaller needles and E, cast on 115 sts.
1st row (RS) K1, (P1, K1) to end.
2nd row P1, (K1, P1) to end.

Rep the last 2 rows twice more, inc one st in centre of last row. 116 sts. Change to larger needles. Beg with a K row, row 1 and working throughout in st st, cont in patt from chart, until 202 rows in all have been worked from top of rib, and chart is complete.

Shape shoulders
Next row Cast/bind off 37 sts, K to last 37 sts, cast/bind off to end. Leave rem 42 sts on a holder for neckband.

FRONT

Work as given for back until 184 rows in all have been worked from top of rib.

Shape neck
Next row Patt 50, turn and leave rem sts on a spare needle.
Next row P2, P2tog tbl, patt to end.
Next row Patt to last 4 sts, sl 1-K1-psso, K2.
Rep the last 2 rows until 37 sts rem. Cont in patt as set, without shaping until 202 rows in all have been worked from top of rib and chart is complete. Cast/bind off.
Return to sts on spare needle; with RS facing, sl first 16 sts on to a holder for neckband, rejoin yarns to neck edge and patt to end.
Next row Patt to last 4 sts, P2tog, P2.
Next row K2, K2tog, patt to end.
Cont to match first side, reversing shaping as set.

SLEEVES

With smaller needles and E, cast on 59 sts and work 6 rows in rib as on back inc one st in centre of last row. 60 sts.
Change to larger needles. Beg with a K row, row 1 and working throughout in st st, cont in patt from chart, working all incs as shown.

NECKBAND

Join right shoulder seam.
With smaller needles, E and RS facing, pick up and K 20 sts evenly down left front neck, K front neck sts from holder, pick up and K 20 sts evenly up right front neck, then K back neck sts from holder inc 3 sts evenly across them. 101 sts.
Beg with a 2nd row, work 6 rows in rib as on back. Cast/bind off *loosely* in rib.

FINISHING

Press pieces lightly as instructed on yarn label, avoiding ribbing. Join left shoulder and neckband seam. Sew in sleeves, with centre of sleeve to shoulder seam. Join side and sleeve seams. Press seams. Sew in shoulder pads.

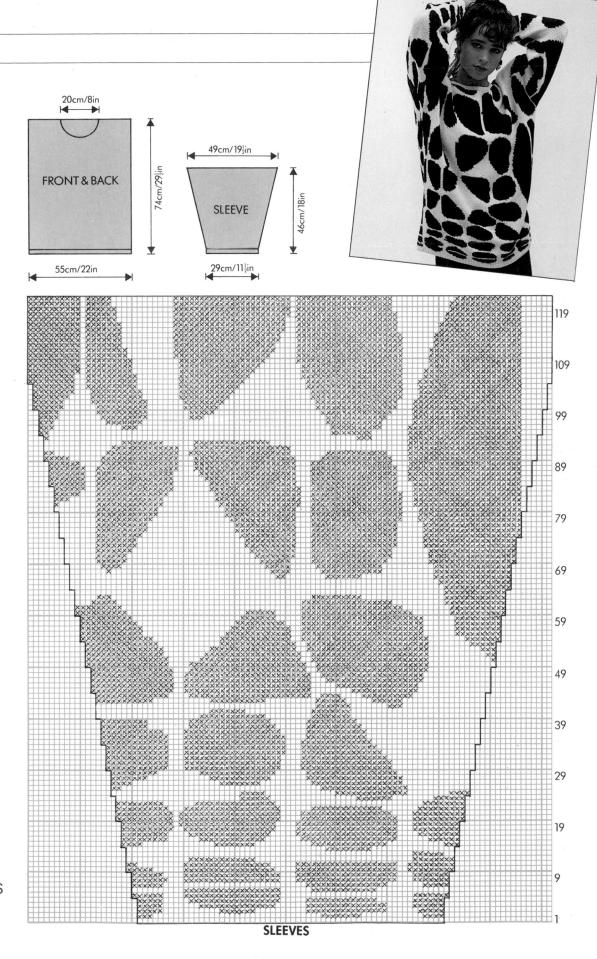

FRONT & BACK

20cm/8in

74cm/29½in

55cm/22in

SLEEVE

49cm/19½in

46cm/18in

29cm/11½in

119
109
99
89
79
69
59
49
39
29
19
9
1

KEY TO CHARTS
E = □ = Ecru
B = x = Black

SLEEVES

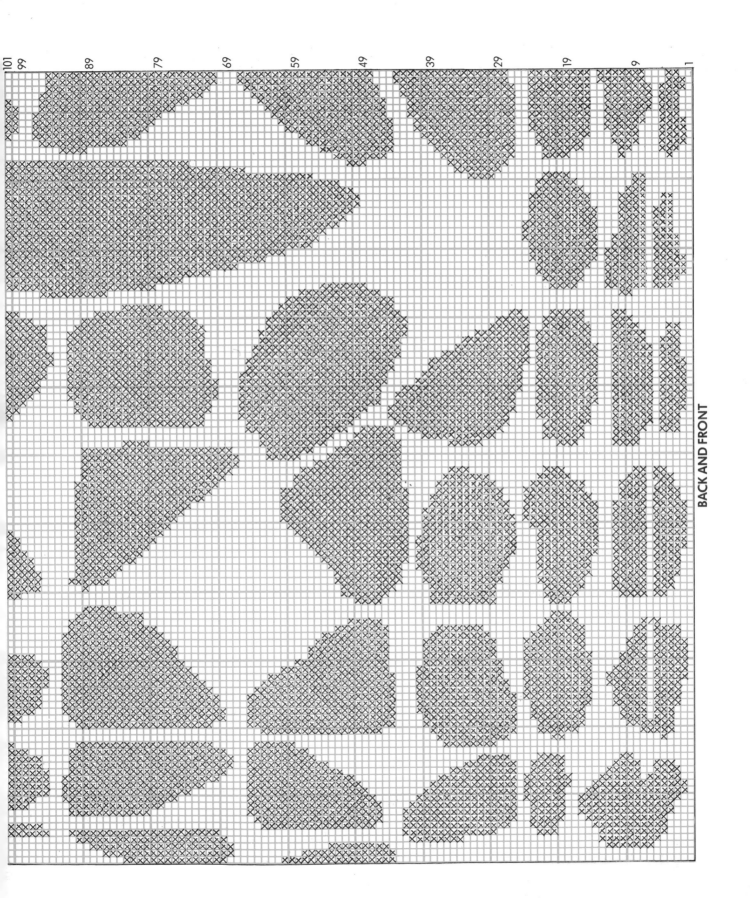

BACK AND FRONT

MINI SKIRT

MATERIALS

7(7:8:8)×50g/1¾oz balls of Anny Blatt *Bora Bora Stranded Cotton.*
1 pair each of 3¼mm/US size 3 and 4mm/US size 6 knitting needles.
Waist length of 2.5cm/1in wide elastic.

SIZES

To fit 81(86:91:97)cm/ 32(34:36:38)in hips.
See diagram for finished measurements.

TENSION/GAUGE

23 sts and 28 rows to 10cm/4in over st st on 4mm/US size 6 needles.

ABBREVIATIONS

See page 11.

BACK AND FRONT (alike)

With smaller needles, cast on 111(117:123:129)sts.
1st row RS K1, [P1, K1] to end.
2nd row P1, [K1, P1] to end.
Rep the last 2 rows twice more.
Change to larger needles. Beg with a K row, cont in st st until skirt measures 36cm/14¼in from beg, ending with a P row.

Shape top
Next row K2, K2tog, K to last 4 sts, sl 1-K1-psso, K2.
Beg with a P row, work 7 rows in st
Rep with last 8 rows 5 times more.

Waistband
Change to smaller needles.
Next row P to end.
Beg with a 2nd row work 6cm/ 2½in in rib as at beg. Cast/bind off *loosely* in rib.

FINISHING

Press pieces lightly as instructed on yarn label, avoiding ribbing.

Join side seams. Fold waistband in half to WS and sew in place, leaving a small opening for elastic. Thread elastic through waistband and join to form a circle. Sew up opening. Press seams.

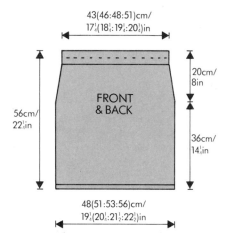

43(46:48:51)cm/ 17¼(18¼:19¼:20¼)in

20cm/ 8in

FRONT & BACK

56cm/ 22¼in

36cm/ 14¼in

48(51:53:56)cm/ 19¼(20¼:21¼:22½)in

LAINEY

◆ MARCUS ◆

Lainey's bold sweater is an adaptable design which can be knitted in a wide variety of novelty bouclé yarns against a plainer background. To match the quantities given here, try to choose a pure wool yarn; synthetics will weigh much less for a similar total length so you will not require quite as much total weight if you use them. Try knitting a front and a sleeve to work out the exact quantity.

MATERIALS

900g/32oz pure wool medium heavy weight yarn in main colour M
350g/12oz pure wool medium heavy weight yarn in contrasting colour C
1×25g/1oz ball of pure DK weight mohair in each of 5 colours
1 pair each of 5½mm/US size 9 and 6mm/US size 10 knitting needles

SIZE

To fit 86-97cm/34-38in bust.
See diagram for finished measurements.

TENSION/GAUGE

29 sts and 20 rows to 10cm/4in over st st on 6mm/US size 10 needles.

Note Use a separate length of yarn for each section and twist yarns together on wrong side of every row to avoid a hole. Read odd numbered rows K from right to left and even numbered rows P from left to right.

ABBREVIATIONS

See page 11.

BACK

With smaller needles and M, cast on 78 sts.
Foundation row (RS) [K1 tbl] to end.
1st row P2, [K2, P2] to end.
2nd row K2, [P2, K2] to end.
Rep the last 2 rows once more.
Next row Rib 7, inc in next st, [rib 2, inc in next st] 21 times, rib to end. 100 sts.
Change to larger needles. Beg with a K row, work 4 rows in st st in M, then 2 rows garter stitch in C. Keeping this sequence of yarn and stitches as background throughout, beg with row 7 cont in patt from chart until 130 rows in all have been worked from top of rib.

Shape shoulders
Cast/bind off 35 sts at beg of next two rows. Leave rem 30 sts on a holder for neckband.

FRONT

Work as given for back until 124 rows in all have been worked from top of rib.

Shape neck
Next row Patt 40, turn and leave rem sts on a spare needle.
Dec one st at neck edge on next 5 rows. Cast/bind off.
Return to sts on spare needle; with RS facing, sl first 20 sts on to a holder for neckband, rejoin yarns to neck edge and patt to end. Cont to match first side, reversing shaping.

SLEEVES

With smaller needles and M, cast on 34 sts and work first 5 rows as on back.
Next row Rib 1, inc in next st, [rib 1, inc in next st] 15 times, rib to end. 50 sts.
Change to larger needles. Beg with a K row cont in st st, inc one st at each end of the 3rd and every foll alternate row until there are 90 sts, then every foll 4th row until there are 104 sts. Cont without shaping until sleeve measures 40cm/15¾in from beg, ending with a P row. Cast/bind off *loosely*.

NECKBAND

Join left shoulder seam.
With larger needles, M and RS facing, K back neck sts from holder, pick up and K 14 sts evenly down left front neck, K front neck sts from holder, then pick up and K 14 sts evenly up right front neck. 78 sts.
Rep first and 2nd rows on back 5 times. Cast/bind off *loosely* in rib.

FINISHING

Do not press.
Join right shoulder and neckband seam. Sew in sleeves, with centre of sleeve to shoulder seam. Join side and sleeve seams.

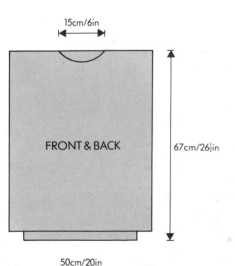

15cm/6in

FRONT & BACK

67cm/26½in

50cm/20in

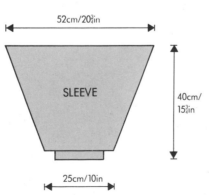

52cm/20¾in

SLEEVE

40cm/15¾in

25cm/10in

KEY TO CHART
Nos 1-5 = Mohair yarn in any order of colour

Lainey

Lainey Keogh works in a tiny office among the antique shops in the heart of Dublin, and also shows her work at the Galeria of Fashion on St Stephen's Green. She taught herself all about knitting as a teenager, and was constantly asked for hand-knits by her friends in the pop and fashion world. Three years ago she set up her business, and was immediately asked by one of Ireland's leading designers, Michael Mortell, to design a knitwear range for him. In 1985 Lainey won the National Knitwear Award.

Lainey's bold colourings and big shapes are dramatic and original without being hard to wear. She believes that hand-knitters need to try to work more individually – she chose these popular designs from her collection so that anyone, with a little imagination, could re-think them in other wools to achieve different effects.

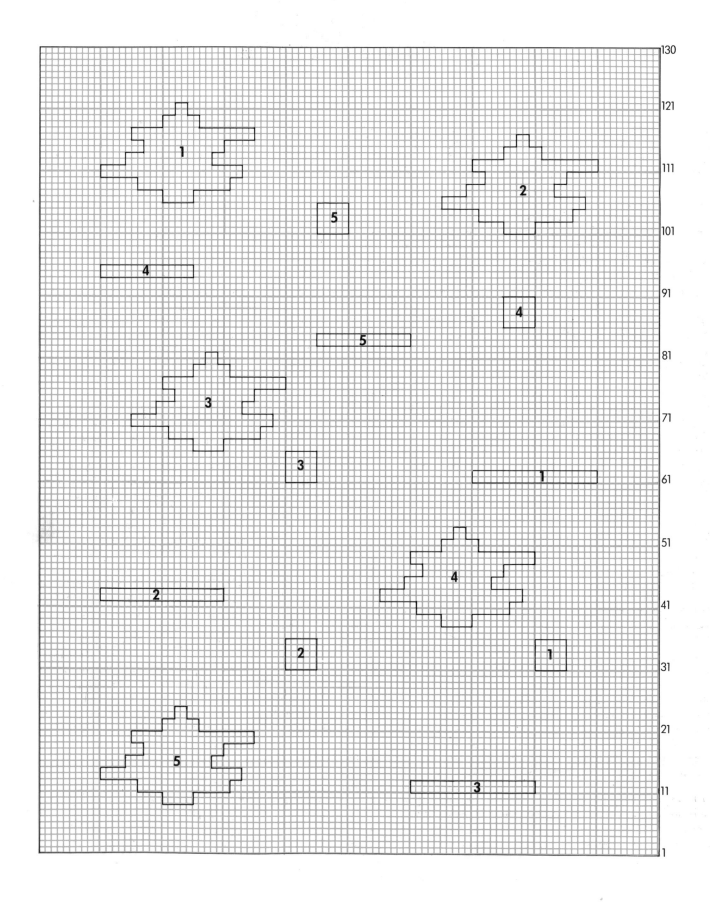

• MOBILE REDS •

Lainey's dramatic cardigan is made in a medium heavy weight mohair, available in a variety of makes and colours. If you vary the colour scheme, emulate her use of two closely related reds and a bold contrast colour for the bobbles. The cardigan is designed to have a little firmness and structure by using a matching medium heavy weight plain wool yarn to make the borders.

MATERIALS

8×25g/1oz balls of medium heavy weight mohair in first colour A (Purple)
8 balls in second colour B (Pink)
5 balls in third colour C (Red)
3 balls in fourth colour (Blue)
2×50g/1¾oz balls of medium heavy weight yarn E
1 pair each of 5mm/US size 8 and 6mm/US size 10 knitting needles
2 buttons

SIZE

To fit 86-102cm/34-40in bust. See diagram for finished measurements.

TENSION/GAUGE

16 sts and 16 rows to 10cm/4in over st st on 6mm/US size 10 needles.

Note Use a separate length of yarn for each section and twist yarns together on every row to avoid a hole. Read odd numbered rows K from right to left and even numbered rows P from left to right.

ABBREVIATIONS

MB – With Blue mohair, [K1, P1, K1, P1, K1] all into next st, turn, P5, turn, K5, turn, P5, turn K5, turn, P5, turn, K5tog. Sl st back on to left hand needle, with A, K it, break and secure Blue yarn before continuing. Cont in A.
Also see page 11.

BACK

With smaller needles and E, cast on 69 sts.
Foundation row [K1 tbl] to end.
1st row K1, [P1, K1] to end.
2nd row P1, [K1, P1] to end.
Rep the last 2 rows once more, then first row again inc one st in centre of last row. 70 sts.
*Change to larger needles. Beg with a K row and working in st st throughout, cont in patt from chart, working all shaping as shown. *

LEFT FRONT

With smaller needles and E, cast on 35 sts and work foundation row as on back.
1st row K1, [P1, K1] to end.
2nd row P1, [K1, P1] to end.
Rep the last 2 rows once more, then first row again.
Read as * to * on back.

RIGHT FRONT

Read as given for left front reversing all shapings to match left front as shown on chart.

SLEEVES

With smaller needles and E, cast on 35 sts and work foundation row as on back.
1st row P1, [K1, P1] to end.
2nd row K1, [P1, K1] to end.
Rep the last 2 rows once more, then first row again inc 15 sts evenly across the last row. 50 sts.
Read as * to * on back.

SHOULDER TOPS (make 2)

With larger needles and E, cast on 31 sts.
Rep first and 2nd rows on sleeves until work measures 10cm/4in from beg. Cast/bind off in rib.

FRONT BAND

Sew cast on edges of shoulder tops to cast/bound off sts at either side of back and cast/bound off edges of shoulder tops to cast/bound off edge of both fronts, sew side edges to sides of centre back piece as far as possible.
With pins mark positions of buttonholes on right front edge, first to come 2cm/¾in from cast on edge, and 2nd to come 16cm/6¼in from same edge.
With smaller needles and E, cast on 12 sts and cont in single rib until band, when slightly stretched, reaches up left front edge, around back neck and down right front edge, making buttonholes to correspond with positions of pins as foll:
(RS) Rib 5, cast/bind off 2, rib to end.
Next row Rib to end, casting on 2 sts over the 2 cast/bound off.

SIDE EDGES (make 2)

Join straight edges of side seams. With smaller needles, E and RS facing, pick up and K 57 sts evenly along shaped edges of back and front. Beg with a 2nd row, work 5 rows in rib as on back. Cast/bind off in rib.

FINISHING

Do not press.
Sew in sleeves. Join sleeve seams.
Sew on front band. Sew on buttons.

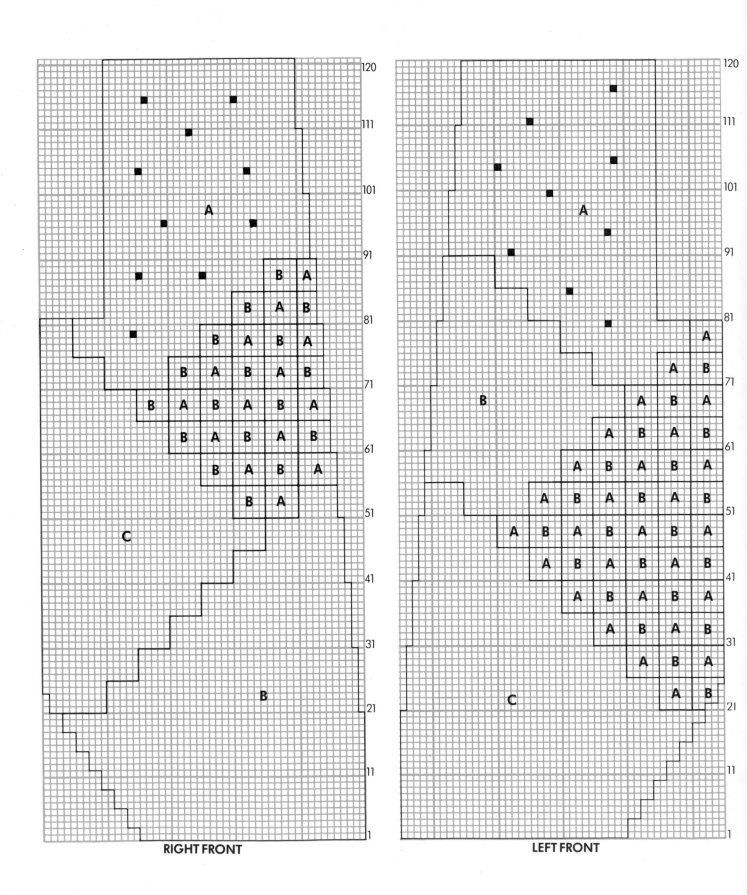

RIGHT FRONT   **LEFT FRONT**

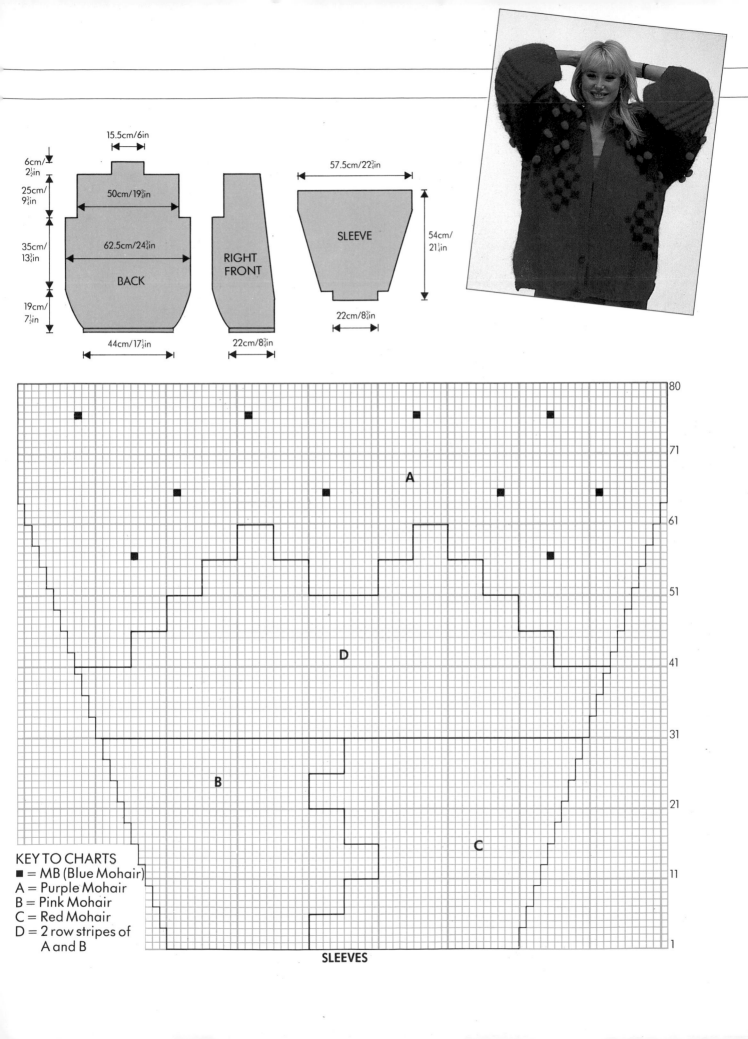

15.5cm/6in

6cm/
2½in

25cm/
9¾in

50cm/19¾in

35cm/
13¾in

62.5cm/24¾in

BACK

RIGHT
FRONT

19cm/
7½in

44cm/17½in

22cm/8¾in

57.5cm/22¾in

SLEEVE

54cm/
21¼in

22cm/8¾in

80

71

A

61

51

D

41

31

B

21

C

11

KEY TO CHARTS
■ = MB (Blue Mohair)
A = Purple Mohair
B = Pink Mohair
C = Red Mohair
D = 2 row stripes of
     A and B

1

SLEEVES

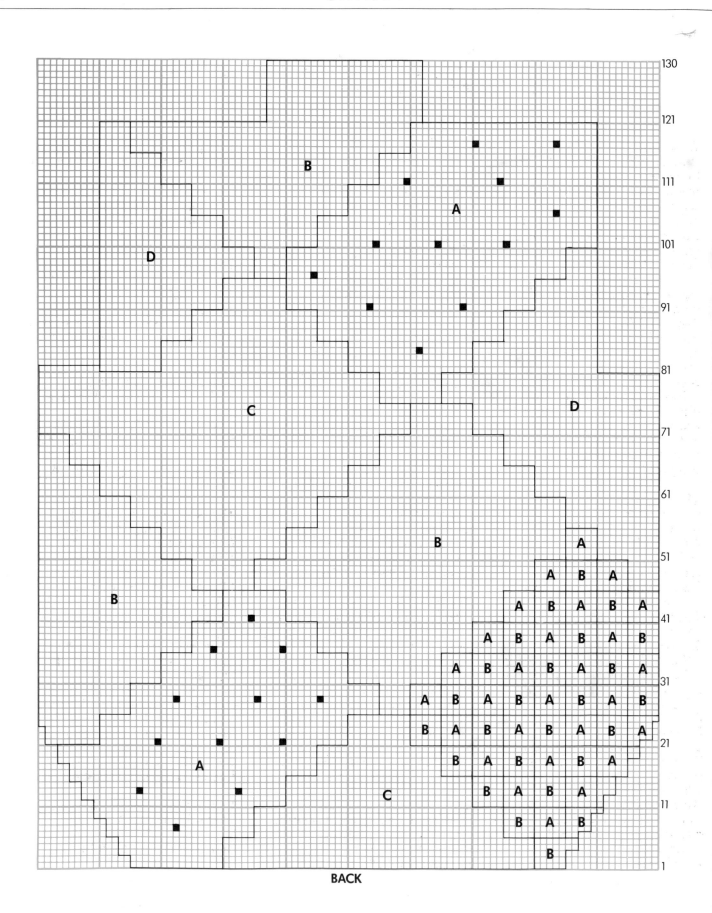

· ICE CREAM SAMPLERS ·

These three designs by Carol Horn show her skill in planning a pattern to suit different figure types, and reveal how altering blocks of colour can give you a totally different look. Each pattern has been carefully varied at the neck and shoulder to balance the different lengths of rib, one for a short cropped top, the second for a hip-length sweater, and the third for a skinny-rib dress. Twilley's *Pegasus 8-Ply Cotton* has a good range of pastels for these designs, but there is no limit to the alternatives you could devise yourself.

The little blocks of 'sample stitches' are just right for the knitter who wants to try out new techniques but would be daunted by a whole garment in a complicated variation.

MATERIALS

Dress
4(4:4)×100g/3½oz balls of Twilley's *Pegasus 8 ply Cotton* in first colour A (Beige)
2(3:3) balls in second colour B (Salmon)
2(2:2) balls in third colour C (White)
Sleeveless top
2(2:2) balls in first colour A (Lilac)
2(3:3) balls in second colour B (Green)
2(2:2) balls in third colour C (White)
Pullover
2(2:2) balls in first colour A (Blue)
3(3:4) balls in second colour B (White)
2(2:2) balls in third colour C (Turquoise)
1 pair each of 3¾mm/US size 5 and 4½mm/US size 7 knitting needles
1 cable needle

SIZES

To fit 86(91:97)cm/34(36:38)in bust.
See diagrams for finished measurements.

TENSION/GAUGE

18 sts and 26 rows to 10cm/4in over st st on 4½mm/US size 7 needles.

Note Use a separate length of yarn for each section and twist yarns together on the wrong side of work on every row to avoid a hole.

For further information on using colours, see the Technical Section, pages 117-18.

ABBREVIATIONS

Tw2togK – sl next 2 sts to cable needle to front of work, sl the first of these sts back on to left hand needle behind cable needle and second st on to right hand needle, K2tog, then psso the K2tog and off right hand needle.
Tw2togP – sl next 2 sts to cable needle to back of work, sl the first of these sts back on to left hand needle in front of cable needle and second st on to right hand needle, P2tog, then psso the P2tog and off right hand needle.
C4 – sl next 2 sts to cable needle to back of work, K2, then K2 from cable needle.
yfwd – yarn forward to front of work between needles then over right hand needle to form a new loop.
yrn – yarn to back of work over right hand needle, around needle and to front of work between needles to form a new loop.
Also see page 11.

PANEL 1

(9 sts, worked throughout in B)
1st row K1, P1, K1, P6.
2nd row K5, P2, K1, P1.
3rd row K1, P1, K3, P4.
4th row K3, P4, K1, P1.
5th row K1, P1, K5, P2.
6th row K1, P6, K1, P1.
These 6 rows form the rep of patt.

PANEL 2

(10 sts, worked throughout in C)
1st row K1, yfwd, sl 1-K1-psso, K6, P1.
2nd row K1, P5, P2tog tbl, yrn, P2.
3rd row K3, yfwd, sl 1-K1-psso, K4, P1.
4th row K1, P3, P2tog tbl, yrn, P4.
5th row K5, yfwd, sl 1-K1-psso, K2, P1.
6th row K1, P1, P2tog tbl, yrn, P6.
7th row K7, yfwd, sl 1-K1 psso, P1.
8th row K1, P2, yrn, P2tog, P5.
9th row K4, K2tog, yfwd, K3, P1.
10th row K1, P4, yrn, P2tog, P3.
11th row K2, K2tog, yfwd, K5, P1.
12th row K1, P6, yrn, P2tog, P1.
These 12 rows from the rep of patt.

PANEL 3

(17sts, worked throughout in B)
1st row: K17.
2nd row K7, P1, K1, P1, K7.
3rd row P6, K1, [P1, K1] twice, P6.
4th row K6, P1, [K1, P1] twice, K6.
5th row P5, K1, [P1, K1] 3 times, P5.
6th row K5, P1, [K1, P1] 3 times, K5.
7th row P4, K1, [P1, K1] 4 times, P4.
8th row K4, P1, [K1, P1] 4 times, K4.
9th row P3, K1, [P1, K1] 5 times, P3.
10th row K3, P1, [K1, P1] 5 times, K3.

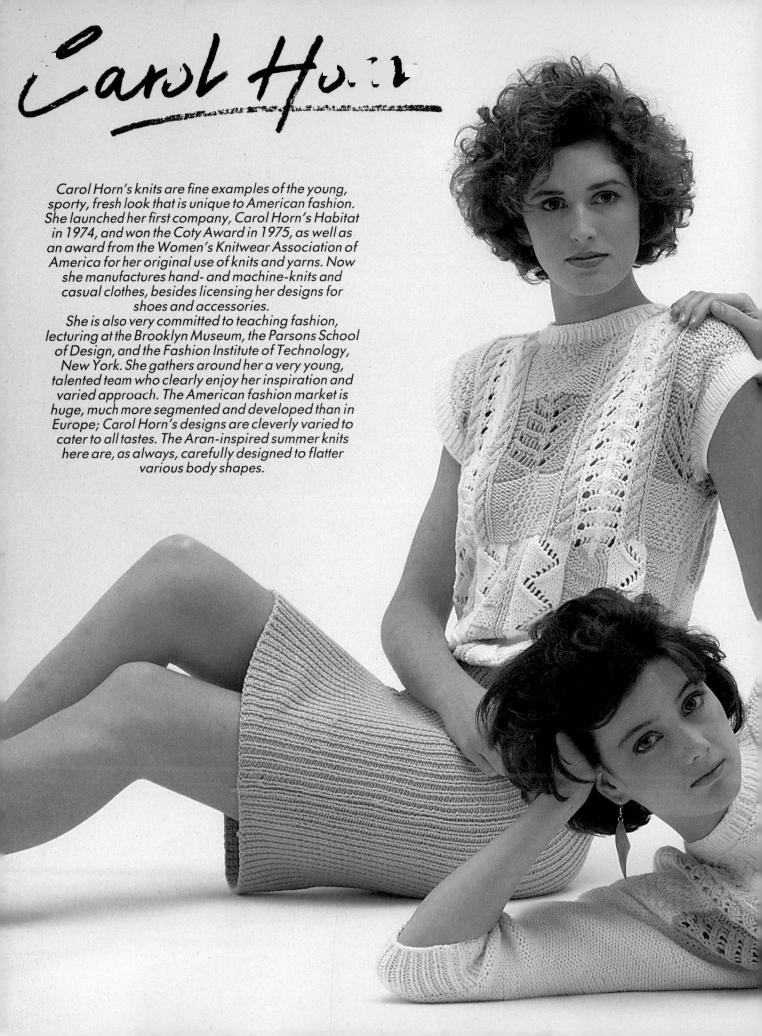

Carol Horn

Carol Horn's knits are fine examples of the young, sporty, fresh look that is unique to American fashion. She launched her first company, Carol Horn's Habitat in 1974, and won the Coty Award in 1975, as well as an award from the Women's Knitwear Association of America for her original use of knits and yarns. Now she manufactures hand- and machine-knits and casual clothes, besides licensing her designs for shoes and accessories.

She is also very committed to teaching fashion, lecturing at the Brooklyn Museum, the Parsons School of Design, and the Fashion Institute of Technology, New York. She gathers around her a very young, talented team who clearly enjoy her inspiration and varied approach. The American fashion market is huge, much more segmented and developed than in Europe; Carol Horn's designs are cleverly varied to cater to all tastes. The Aran-inspired summer knits here are, as always, carefully designed to flatter various body shapes.

11th row As 7th row.
12th row As 8th row.
13th row As 5th row.
14th row As 6th row.
15th row As 3rd row.
16th row As 4th row.
17th row P7, K1, P1, K1, P7.
18th row As 2nd row.

PANEL 4

(23 sts)
1st row With B, K1, P1, K4, with C, K1, yfwd, K3, Tw2togK, K3, yfwd, K1, with B, K4, P1, K1.
2nd row Working in colours as set, P1, K1, P6, yrn, P2, Tw2togP, P2, yrn, P6, K1, P1.
3rd row Working in colours as set, K1, P1, C4, K3, yfwd, K1, Tw2togK, K1, yfwd, K3, C4, P1, K1.
4th row: Working in colours as set, P1, K1, P8, yrn, Tw2togP, yrn, P8, K1, P1.
These 4 rows form the rep of patt.

PANEL 5

(17 sts, worked throughout in A)
1st row K17.
2nd row K6, P2tog tbl, yrn, P1, yrn, P2tog, K6.
3rd row P5, K2tog, yfwd, K3, yfwd, sl 1-K1-psso, P5.
4th row K4, P2tog tbl, yrn, P5, yrn, P2tog, K4.
5th row P3, K2tog, yfwd, K7, yfwd, sl 1-K1-psso, P3.
6th row K2, P2tog tbl, yrn, P2, P2tog tbl, yrn, P1, yrn, P2tog, P2, yrn, P2tog, K2.
7th row P1, K2tog, yfwd, K2, K2tog, yfwd, K3, yfwd, sl 1-K1-psso, K2, yfwd, sl1-K1-psso, P1.
8th row P2tog tbl, yrn, P2, P2tog tbl, yrn, P5, yrn, P2tog, P2, yrn, P2tog.
9th row As 5th row.
10th row As 6th row.
11th row As 7th row.
12th row As 4th row.
13th row As 5th row.
14th row As 6th row.
15th row As 3rd row.
16th row As 4th row.
17th row As 5th row.

18th row As 2nd row.
19th row As 3rd row.
20th row As 4th row.

PANEL 6

(17 sts, worked throughout in B)
1st row K17.
2nd row K7, P1, K1, P1, K7.
3rd row P6, K1, [P1, K1] twice, P6.
4th row K6, P1, [K1, P1] twice, K6.
5th row P5, K1, [P1, K1] 3 times, P5.
6th row K5, P1, [K1, P1] 3 times, K5.
7th row P4, [K1, P1] twice, P1, [P1, K1] twice, P4.
8th row K4 [P1, K1] twice, K1, [K1, P1] twice, K4.
9th row P3, [K1, P1] twice, P3, [P1, K1] twice, P3.
10th row K3, [P1, K1] twice, K3, [K1, P1] twice, K3.
11th row As 7th row.
12th row As 8th row.
13th row As 5th row.
14th row As 6th row.
15th row As 3rd row.
16th row As 4th row.
17th row P7, K1, P1, K1, P7.
18th row As 2nd row.

DRESS

BACK AND FRONT (alike)

With smaller needles and A, cast on 79(83:87)sts.
1st row (RS) K1, [P1, K1] to end.
2nd row P1, [K1, P1] to end.
Rep the last 2 rows until dress measures 51(52:53)cm/ 20(20½:21)in from beg, ending with a 2nd row and inc 10 sts evenly across the last row. 89(93:97)sts.
Break off A.
Change to larger needles and cont in patt as foll:
1st row K 2(4:6)B, [with B, K1, P1, K7, work 10 sts as first row of Panel 2] 4 times, with B, K1, P1, K to end.
2nd row P2(4:6)B, [work 9 sts as 2nd row of Panel 1, work 10 sts as 2nd row of Panel 2] 4 times, work 9

sts as 2nd row of Panel 1, P 2(4:6)B.
This sets position of panels.
Keeping panel sts correct as set and sts at each end in st st and B, cont until 54 rows in all have been worked from top of rib.
55th row With B, K 19(21:23), *with C, K1, yfwd, K3, Tw2togK, K3, yfwd, K1, * with B, K29; rep from * to * once, with B, K to end.
56th row With B, K 3(5:7), P1, K1, P1, K7, work 23 sts as 2nd row of Panel 4, work 17 sts as 2nd row of Panel 3, work 23 sts as 2nd row of Panel 4, with B, K7, P1, K1, P1, K to end.
This sets position of panels.
Keeping panel sts correct as set, cont as foll:
57th row With B, P 2(4:6), K1, [P1, K1] twice, P6, patt to last 13(15:17)sts, with B, P6, K1 [P1, K1] twice, P to end.
58th row With B, K 2(4:6), P1, [K1, P1] twice, K6, patt to last 13(15:17)sts, with B, K6, P1, [K1, P1] twice, K to end.
59th row With B, P 1(3:5), K1, [P1, K1] 3 times, P5, patt to last 13(15:17)sts, with B, P5, K1, [P1, K1] 3 times, P to end.
60th row With B, K 1(3:5), P1, [K1, P1] 3 times, K5, patt to last 13(15:17)sts, with B, K5, P1, [K1, P1] 3 times, K to end.
61st row With B, P 0(2:4), K1, [P1, K1] 4 times, P4, patt to last 13(15:17)sts, with B, P4, K1, [P1, K1] 4 times, P 0(2:4).
62nd row With B, K 0(2:4), P1, [K1,P1] 4 times, K4, patt to last 13(15:17)sts, with B, K4, P1, [K1, P1] 4 times, K 0(2:4).
63rd row With B, P 0(1:3), K 0(1:1), [P1, K1] 5 times, P3, patt to last 13(15:17)sts, with B, P3, [K1, P1] 5 times, K 0(1:1), P 0(1:3).
64th row With B, K 0(1:3), P 0(1:1), [K1, P1] 5 times, K3, patt to last 13(15:17)sts, with B, K3, [P1, K1] 5 times, P 0(1:1), K 0(1:3).
65th row Read as 61st row.
66th row Read as 62nd row.
67th row Read as 59th row.
68th row Read as 60th row.
69th row read as 57th row.

70th row Read as 58th row.
71st row With B, P 3(5:7), K1, P1, K1, P7, patt to last 13(15:17)sts, with B, P7, K1, P1, P to end.
72nd row With B, K 3(5:7), P1, K1, P1, K7, patt to last 13(15:17)sts, with B, K7, P1, K1, P1, K to end.
73rd row With A, K 13(15:17), patt 23 sts as set, K 17, patt 23 sts as set, with A, K to end.
74th row With A, K 2(4:6), P2tog tbl, yrn, P1, yrn, P2tog, K6, patt 23 sts as set, work 17 sts as 2nd row of Panel 5, patt 23 sts as set, with A, K6, P2tog tbl, yrn, P1, yrn, P2tog, K to end.
This sets position of panels.
Keeping panel sts correct as set, cont as foll:
75th row With A, P 1(3:5), K2tog, yfwd, K3, yfwd, sl 1-K1-psso, P5, patt to last 13(15:17)sts, with A, P5, K2tog, yfwd, K3, yfwd, sl 1-K1-psso, P to end.
76th row With A, K 0(2:4), P2tog tbl, yrn, P5, yrn, P2tog, K4, patt to last 13(15:17)sts, with A, K4, P2tog tbl, yrn, P5, yrn, P2tog, K 0(2:4).
77th row With A, P 0(1:3), [K2tog, yfwd] 0(1:1) time, K 8(7:7), yfwd, sl 1-K1-psso, P3, patt to last 13(15:17)sts, with A, P3, K2tog, yfwd, K 8(7:7), [yfwd, sl 1-K1-psso] 0(1:1) time, P 0(1:3).
78th row With A, K 0(0:2), [P2tog tbl, yrn] 0(1:1) time, P2, P2tog tbl, yrn, P1, yrn, P2tog, P2, yrn, P2tog, K2, patt to last 13(15:17)sts, with A, K2, P2tog tbl, yrn, P2, P2tog tbl, yrn, P1, yrn, P2tog, P2, [yrn, P2tog] 0(1:1) time, K 0(0:2).
79th row With A, P 0(0:1), [K2tog, yfwd] 0(0:1) time, K 1(3:2), K2tog, yfwd, K3, yfwd, sl 1-K1-psso, K2, yfwd, sl 1-K1-psso, P1, patt to last 13(15:17)sts, with A, P1, K2tog, yfwd, K2, K2tog, yfwd, K3, yfwd, sl 1-K1-psso, K 1(3:2), [yfwd, sl 1-K1-psso] 0(0:1) time, P 0(0:1).
80th row With A, [P2tog, tbl, yrn] 0(0:1) time, P 0(2:2), P2tog tbl, yrn, P5, yrn, P2tog, P2, yrn, P2tog, patt to last 13(15:17)sts, with A, P2tog tbl, yrn, P2, P2tog tbl, yrn, P5, yrn, P2tog, P 0(2:2), [yrn, P2tog]

0(0:1) time.
81st row Read as 77th row.
82nd row Read as 78th row.
83rd row Read as 79th row.
84th row Read as 76th row.
85th row Read as 77th row.
86th row Read as 78th row.
87th row Read as 75th row.
88th row Read as 76th row.
89th row Read as 77th row.
90th row Read as 74th row.
91st row Read as 75th row.
92nd row Read as 76th row.
93rd row With B, K 13(15:17), patt 23 sts as set, K 17, patt 23 sts as set, with B, K to end.
94th row With B, K 3(5:7), P1, K1, P1, K7, patt 23 sts as set, work 17 sts as 2nd row of Panel 6, patt 23 sts as set, with B, K7, P1, K1, P1, K to end.
This sets position of panels.
Keeping panel sts correct as set, cont as foll:
95th-98th rows Read as 57th-60th rows.
99th row With B, P 0(2:4), [K1, P1] twice, P1, [P1, K1] twice, P4, patt to last 13(15:17)sts, with B, P4, [K1, P1] twice, P1, [P1, K1] twice, P 0(2:4).
100th row With B, K 0(2:4), [P1, K1] twice, K1, [K1, P1] twice, K4, patt to last 13(15:17)sts, with B, K4, [P1, K1] twice, K1, [K1, P1] twice, K 0(2:4).
101st row With B, P 0(1:3), K 0(1:1), P1, K1, P4, [P1, K1] twice, P3, patt to last 13(15:17)sts, with B, P3, [K1, P1] twice, P4, K1, P1, K 0(1:1), P 0(1:3).
102nd row With B, K 0(1:3), P 0(1:1), K1, P1, K4, [K1, P1] twice, K3, patt to last 13(15:17)sts, with B, K3, [P1, K1] twice, K4, P1, K1, P 0(1:1), K 0(1:3).
103rd row Read as 99th row.
104th row Read as 100th row.
105th row Read as 59th row.
106th row Read as 60th row.
107th row read as 57th row.
108th row Read as 58th row.
109th row Read as 71st row.
110th row Read as 72nd row.
111th row With B, P 13(15:17), K23, P17, K23, P to end.

Shape neck
Working throughout in B:
112th row P 30(32:34), turn and leave rem sts on a spare needle. Purling every row, dec one st at neck edge on next 8 rows. Cast/bind off.
** Return to sts on spare needle; with WS facing, sl first 29 sts on to a holder for neckband, rejoin B to neck edge and P to end. Cont to match first side, reversing shaping.

NECKBAND

Join right shoulder seam.
With smaller needles, C and RS facing, pick up and K 10 sts evenly down left front neck, K front neck sts from holder, pick up and K 9 sts evenly up right front neck and 9 sts down right back neck, K back neck sts from holder, then pick up and K 9 sts evenly up left back neck. 95 sts. Beg with a 2nd row, work 7 rows in rib as on body. Cast/bind off *loosely*.

ARMHOLE BORDERS

Join left shoulder and neckband seam.
* Place a marker on each side of back and front 20(21:22)cm/ 7¾(8¼:8¾)in down from shoulder. With smaller needles, C and RS facing pick up and K 97(101:105)sts evenly between markers.
Beg with a 2nd row, work 9 rows in rib as on body. Cast/bind off *loosely*.

FINISHING

Do not press. Join side seams and ends of armhole borders.

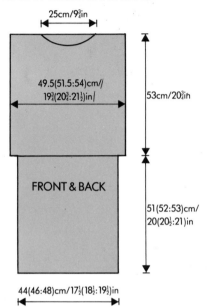

25cm/9¾in

49.5(51.5:54)cm/
19¾(20¾:21½)in

53cm/20¾in

FRONT & BACK

51(52:53)cm/
20(20½:21)in

44(46:48)cm/17½(18½:19½)in

PULLOVER

BACK AND FRONT (alike)

With smaller needles and A, cast on 89(93:97)sts and work 8(9:10)cm/3(3½:4)in in rib as on dress, ending with a 2nd row. Break off A. Change to larger needles and cont in patt as foll:
1st row With C, K 1(3:5), P1, [with B, K1, P1, K7, work 10 sts as first row of Panel 2] 4 times, with B, K1, P1, K7, with C, K2 (4:6).
2nd row With C, P 2(4:6), [work 9 sts as 2nd row of Panel 1, work 10 sts as 2nd row of Panel 2] 4 times, work 9 sts as 2nd row of Panel 1, with C, K1, P to end.
This sets position of panels. Keeping panel sts correct as set and sts at each end in C, cont until 24 rows in all have been worked from top of rib.
25th-81st rows Work as rows 55-111 on dress.

Shape neck
Working throughout in B:

82nd row P 30(32:34), turn and leave rem sts on a spare needle. Purling every row, dec one st at neck edge on next 8 rows. Cast/bind off.
Work as given for dress from ** to end.

NECKBAND

As given for dress.

SLEEVES

With smaller needles and B, cast on 45(47:49)sts and work 5cm/2in in rib as on dress, ending with a 2nd row. Change to larger needles. Beg with a P row, cont in reverse st st inc one st at each end of the 5th and every foll 4th row until there are 75(79:83)sts. Cont without shaping until sleeve measures 35cm/13¾in from beg, ending with a K row. Cast/bind off *loosely*.

FINISHING

Do not press. Join left shoulder and neckband seam. Sew in sleeves, with centre of sleeve to shoulder seam. Join side and sleeve seams.

42(44:46)cm/16½(17½:18½)in

SLEEVE

30cm/11¾in

5cm/2in

25(26:27)cm/
10(10½:11)in

25cm/9¾in

FRONT & BACK

38cm/15in

8(9:10)cm/
3(3½:4)in

49.5(51.5:54)cm/19¾(20¾:21½)in

SLEEVELESS TOP

BACK AND FRONT (alike)

With smaller needles and A, cast on 89(93:97)sts and work 12(13:14)cm/4¾(5:5½)in in rib as on dress, ending with a 2nd row. Break off A. Change to larger needles and cont in patt as foll:
1st row With C, K 1(3:5), P1 [with B, K1, P1, K7, work 10 sts as first row of Panel 2] 4 times, with B, K1, P1, K7, K2 (4:6).
2nd row With C, P2(4:6), [work 9 sts as 2nd row of Panel 1, work 10 sts as 2nd row of Panel 2] 4 times, work 9 sts as 2nd row of Panel 1, with C, K1, P to end.
This sets position of panels. Keeping panel sts correct as set and sts at each end in C, cont until 42 rows in all have been worked from top of rib.
43rd-99th rows Work as rows 55-111 on dress.
Working throughout in B: P 9 rows.

Shape shoulders
P 22(24:26), cast/bind off 29, P to end. Cont on last set of sts only, P one row then cast/bind off.
Return to sts which were left; with WS facing, rejoin B to neck edge and P to end. Cast/bind off.

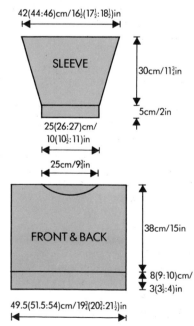

ARMHOLE BORDERS

Join shoulder seams.
Work as given for dress from *to end.

FINISHING

As given for dress.

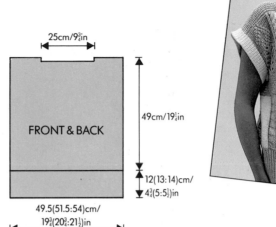

25cm/9¾in

FRONT & BACK

49cm/19¼in

12(13:14)cm/
4¾(5:5½)in

49.5(51.5:54)cm/
19¾(20¾:21½)in

CLAIRE

· LATTICE YOKE CARDIGAN ·

Claire's designs are all very versatile, and build up a wardrobe of interchangeable pieces. She makes them in silk-and-linen yarns, medium weight (4-ply) pure wools, or an equivalent weight in cotton. The examples illustrated are made in a cotton, and the yarn weights are given for this yarn. Measurements are necessarily approximate as the garments are designed to stretch and drape when worn. You can make them longer or shorter to suit your own design.

MATERIALS

A total of 400g/14oz of a lightweight cotton yarn in main colour A
25g/1oz of a lightweight cotton yarn in contrasting colour B
1 pair each of 3¼mm/US size 3 and 4mm/US size 6 knitting needles
1 cable needle
8 small buttons
3mm crochet hook and blunt-pointed needle for embroidery

SIZE

To fit 86-96cm/34-38in bust.
See diagram for finished measurements.

TENSION/GAUGE

22 sts and 28 rows to 10cm/4in over st st on 4mm/US size 6 needles.

ABBREVIATIONS

M1 – pick up loop lying between sts and work into back of it.
C3R – sl next st to cable needle to front of work, sl the 2 slipped sts back on to left hand needle, K1 from cable needle, K2.
C3L – sl next st to cable needle to front of work, K2, then K1 from cable needle.
Also see page 11.

BACK

With smaller needles and A, cast on 99 sts.
1st row (RS) K1, [P1, K1] to end.

2nd row P1, [K1, P1] to end.
Rep the last 2 rows 3 times more, then first row again.
Next row P6, M1, [P1, M1, P2, M1] 29 times, rib to end. 158 sts.
Change to larger needles. Beg with a K row, cont in st st until back measures 33cm/13in from beg, ending with a K row. Place a marker for pocket linings at each end of 28th row in st st. Cont in patt as foll:
1st row P3, [yarn to back of work over right hand needle and to front of work again between needle – called yrn – P1, yrn, P5] to end, ending last rep P4.
2nd row K3, [sl 1 purlwise, drop yrn, sl 1 purlwise, drop yrn, K4] to end, ending last rep K3.
3rd row P3, [sl 2, P4] to end, ending last rep P3.
4th row K3, [sl 2 purlwise, K4] to end, ending last rep K3.
5th row As 3rd row.
6th row K1, [sl 2 purlwise, C3R, C3L] to last st, K1.
7th row P1, [yrn, P5, yrn, P1] to last st, P1.
8th row K1, [sl 1 purlwise, drop

Claire

Claire Oates is a totally original designer who works from her own shop at Barnard Castle, County Durham. After training at Loughborough and Goldsmiths' colleges, she worked as an art therapist before setting up her company in 1982, in rural Teesdale, reviving knitting talents that were traditional to the men lead miners of that area. Her clothes have an earthy, pure beauty to them. She uses only natural fibres, mainly cotton mixes, preferring black, white and oatmeal colours. The appeal of her designs lies in their loose knit, which makes them drape and alter with the individual's shape and movements. Stunning on women – and men – of all ages, they mix together to make a coherent, interchangeable collection.

yrn, K4, sl 1 purlwise, drop yrn] to last st, K1.
9th row P1, sl 1, P4, [sl 2, P4] to last 2 sts, sl 1, P1.
10th row K1, sl 1, K4, [sl 2 purlwise, K4] to last 2 sts, sl 1, K1.
11th row As 9th row.
12th row K1, [C3L, sl 2 purlwise, C3R] to last st, K1.
The last 12 rows form the rep of patt. Work 37 more rows as set.

Shape shoulders
Cast/bind off 67 sts at beg of next 2 rows. Leave rem 24 sts on a holder.

LEFT FRONT

With smaller needles, cast on 55 sts and work 9 rows in rib as on back.
Next row Rib 9 and leave these sts on a safety pin, M1, [P1, M1, P2, M1] 15 times, P1. 77 sts.
Change to larger needles. Beg with a K row work 6 rows in st st.
Next row [K1, P1] twice, K to end.
Next row P to last 4 sts, [K1, P1] twice.
Rep the last 2 rows 10 times more.
Cont in st st until left front measures 33cm/13in from beg, ending with a K row.
Cont in patt as foll:
1st row [P1, yrn, P5, yrn] to last 5 sts, P1, yrn, P4.
2nd row K3, [sl 1 purlwise, drop yrn, sl 1 purlwise, drop yrn, K4] to last 3 sts, sl 1 purlwise, drop yrn, K1.
This sets position of patt. Work 38 more rows as set.

Shape neck
Keeping patt correct, cast/bind off 6 sts at beg of next row, then dec one st at neck edge of next 4 rows. 67 sts.
Work 4 rows without shaping.
Cast/bind off.

RIGHT FRONT

With smaller needles, cast on 55 sts and work 2 rows in rib as on back.
*****Next row** Rib 3, cast/bind off 3, rib to end.
Next row Rib to end, casting on 3

sts over the 3 cast/bound off. *
Work 5 more rows in rib as set.
Next row P1, [M1, P2, M1, P1] 15 times, M1, turn and leave rem 9 sts on a safety pin. 77 sts.
Change to larger needles. Beg with a K row, work 6 rows in st st.
Next row K to last 4 sts, [P1, K1] twice.
Next row [P1, K1] twice, P to end.
Rep the last 2 rows 10 times more.
Cont in st st until right front measures 33cm/13in from beg, ending with a K row.
Cont in patt as foll:
1st row P3, [yrn, P1, yrn, P5] to last 2 sts, yrn, P2.
2nd row K1, [sl 1 purlwise, drop yrn, K4, sl 1 purlwise, drop yrn] to last 5 sts, sl 1 purlwise, drop yrn, K3.
This sets position of patt. Cont to match left front, reversing shaping.

SLEEVES

With smaller needles cast on 37 sts and work 9 rows in rib as on back.
Next row P1, [M1, P1] to end. 73 sts.
Change to larger needles. Beg with a K row, cont in st st, inc one st at each end of the 7th and every foll 6th row until there are 103 sts.
Cont without shaping until sleeve measures 43cm/17in from beg, ending with P row. Cast/bind off *loosely*.

BUTTON BAND

With smaller needles and RS facing, rib across sts on safety pin at beg of left front, working twice into first st. 10 sts.
Cont in rib as set until band, when slightly stretched, reaches up front edge to neck, ending with a WS row.
Leave sts on a holder.
Sew band in place; with pins mark positions of buttons, first to come level with buttonhole already worked, 2nd to come 12 rows down from sts on holder, with 5 more spaced evenly between these 2.

BUTTONHOLE BAND

With smaller needles and WS facing, rib across sts on safety pin at beg of right front, working twice into first st. 10 sts. Cont to match button band, making buttonholes to correspond with position of pins as before. Sew band in place.

NECKBAND

Join shoulder seams.
With smaller needles and RS facing, rib 10 sts from buttonhole band, pick up and K 21 sts evenly up right front neck, K back neck sts from holder inc one st in centre, pick up and K 21 sts evenly down left front neck, then rib across 10 sts on holder. 85 sts.
Work 3 rows in rib as set. Rep from * to * on right front once, then work 4 more rows.
Next row Cast/bind off 9, rib to last 9 sts, cast/bind off to end.
Rejoin yarn to remaining 67 sts and work 9 rows more. Cast/bind off in rib.

POCKET LININGS (make 2)

With larger needles and RS facing, pick up and K 22 sts evenly between top of rib and marker on back. Beg with P row, work 10cm/4in in st st. Cast/bind off.

FINISHING

Press pieces lightly according to instructions on yarn label. Sew in sleeves, with centre of sleeve to shoulder seam. Join side seams, leaving an opening for pocket. Sew down pocket linings. Join sleeve seams. Press seams. Sew on buttons.

EMBROIDERY

Zigzag lines, leaves and stems can be embroidered on using a blunt-pointed needle or worked in double crochet/US single crochet. Make zigzag 2cm/¾in deep.

Using B, work zigzag line from right to left around neck below neckband so that points of zigzags on one side meet rib, then continue down left front, around lower edge and up right front, placing zigzag so that points touch front bands and lower rib. Using B, work a zigzag line around armhole on fronts and back.
Using B, work stems and leaves on fronts and back foll diagram.
Work a straight line on sleeve cuff to form mock placket, beg for 2cm/¾in along cuff edge, then turning and working 12cm/5in up sleeve.
Using B, work dots that form flowers in detached chain stitch or French knots.

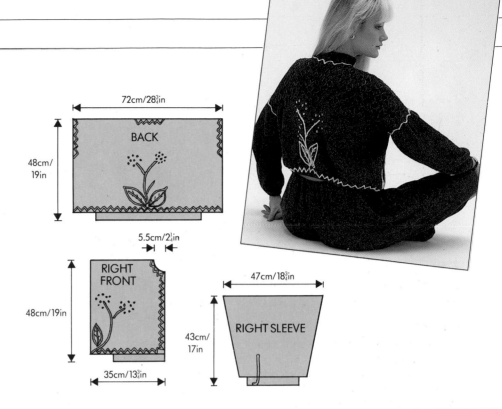

• VOLUMINOUS SWEATER •

MATERIALS

A total of 600g/21oz of medium weight cotton in main colour A (Beige)
A total of 300g/11oz of medium weight cotton in colour B (Black)
1 pair of 4mm/US size 6 knitting needles

SIZE

To fit 86-102cm/34-40in bust. See diagram for finished measurements.

TENSION/GAUGE

23 sts and 28 rows to 10cm/4in over rib on 4mm/US size 6 needles.

ABBREVIATIONS

See page 11.

BACK AND FRONT (alike)

With A, cast on 141 sts.
1st row (RS) K1, [P1, K1] to end.
2nd row P1, [K1, P1] to end.
Rep the last 2 rows 4 times more.
Cont in rib as set, working in stripes of 2 rows B, 4 rows A, 6 rows B, 10 rows A throughout until work measures 54cm/21¼in from beg. Cast/bind off in rib.

SLEEVES (make 4)

With A, cast on 41 sts and cont in rib and stripes as on back, inc one st at each of the 3rd and every foll 4th row until there are 97 sts. Cont without shaping until sleeve measures 41cm/16¼in from beg. Cast/bind off *loosely* in rib.

LOWER PANELS (make 2)

With A, cast on 101 sts and cont in rib and stripes as on back, inc one st at each end of the 3rd and every foll alternate row until there are 111 sts.
Work 91 rows without shaping.
Cast/bind off *loosely* in rib.

GUSSETS (make 2)

With A, cast on 2 sts. Beg with a K row, cont in st st, inc one st at each end of the next and every foll 4th row until there are 50 sts. Work 3 rows without shaping.
Dec one st at each end of the next and every foll 4th row until 2 sts rem.
Cast/bind off.

COLLAR (make 2)

With A, cast on 55 sts and work 40 rows in rib as on back.
Cast/bind off *loosely* in rib.

FINISHING

Do not press. Sew cast/bound off edge of lower panel to row ends of back and front (rib runs sideways). Join shoulder seams, leaving 25cm/10in open for neck. Join straight edges of sleeves to make a pair. Sew top edge of gusset to top of sleeves. Sew in sleeves with centre of sleeve to shoulder seam and lower edge of gusset to side seam. Join side and sleeve seams. Fold each collar piece in half, sew up side seams, turn out to right side. Sew to neck edge, beg and ending each piece at centre front and back.

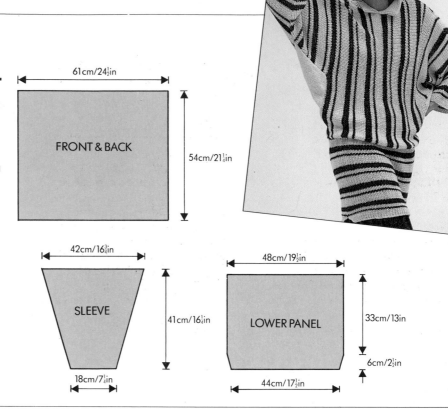

FRONT & BACK
61cm/24½in
54cm/21¼in

SLEEVE
42cm/16¾in
41cm/16¼in
18cm/7¼in

LOWER PANEL
48cm/19½in
33cm/13in
6cm/2½in
44cm/17½in

VIVIENNE BANNISTER

◆ TRELLIS PATTERN SWEATER ◆

Vivienne Bannister's *Trellis Pattern* sweater was knitted in the same yarn as suggested for the *Night Lights* design, and the same advice about applying the sequin trim will help to achieve the best finished effect on this design. Other colourways would look just as lively for this sweater – red on black, black trellis on a dark blue, or deep pink, and so on. Pure mohairs are available in a wide range of suitable colours, but be sure to match the colour of the sequins to the background chain stitch yarn to achieve the best effect.

MATERIALS

16 25g/1oz balls of Argyll's *Finesse* mohair in main colour M (Black)
2×25g/1oz balls of contrasting colour C (Blue)
1 pair each of 3mm/US size 3 and 6mm/US size 10 knitting needles
Approx 15m/16¼yds of blue sequin trim

SIZE

To fit 86-102cm/34-40in bust. See diagram for finished measurements and position of sequin trim.

TENSION/GAUGE

16 sts and 20 rows to 10cm/4in over st st on 6mm/US size 10 needles.

ABBREVIATIONS

See page 11.

BACK AND FRONT (alike)

With smaller needles and M, cast on 89 sts.
1st row (RS) K1, [P1, K1] to end.
2nd row P1, [K1, P1] to end.
Rep the last 2 rows until rib measures 8cm/3¼in from beg, ending with a 2nd row. Change to larger needles. Beg with a K row, cont in st st until back measures 56cm/22in from beg, ending with a P row.
Next row K25, P1, [K1, P1] 19 times, K to end.
Next row P25, K1, [P1, K1] 19 times, P to end.

Rep the last 2 rows once more, then the first of them again.
Next row P25, cast/bind off 39 sts in rib, P to end.
Cont on last set of sts only, work 3 rows in st st. Cast/bind off.
Return to sts which were left; with RS facing, rejoin M to neck edge and K to end. Work 2 rows in st st. Cast/bind off.

SLEEVES

With smaller needles and M, cast on 39 sts and work 8cm/3¼in in rib as on body, ending with a 2nd row and inc one st on centre of last row. 40 sts.
Change to larger needles. Beg with a K row, cont in st st inc one st at each end of the 5th and every foll 6th row until there are 50 sts, every foll 4th row until there are 64 sts, then every foll alternate row until there are 80 sts. Work one row without shaping, then cast/bind off *loosely*.

NECK RIBS (make 2)

Join shoulder seams.
With larger needles, M and RS facing, pick up and K 5 sts evenly along side edge of neck. Work 4 rows in rib as on body. Cast/bind off in rib.

FINISHING

Do not press.
Sew in sleeves, with centre of sleeve to shoulder seam. Using 2 strands of C tog and in chain st, work embroidery following diagram. Sew sequin trim on top of chain stitch (leaving joined in continuous row as purchased) using couching stitch to catch down the strand of sequins. Join side and sleeve seams. Sew ends of neck ribs to cast/bound off edge of neckband at either side.

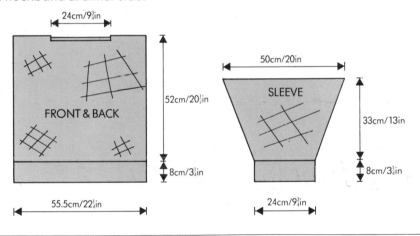

◆ NIGHT LIGHTS ◆

Vivienne Bannister's designs are full of humour and very bold in shape and decoration. She uses Argyll's *Finesse*, but other medium heavy weight pure mohairs can be used. For the sequin embroidery, use the strips as they are purchased – do not try to sew them on individually as they will have no impact against the thick fluff of a pure mohair. Also, Vivienne recommends brushing up the finished knitting, so that the colour of the yarn used for the chain stitch behind the sequins forms a halo effect, softening the brilliance of the trim a little.

MATERIALS

12×25g/1oz balls of Argyll's *Finesse* mohair in main colour M (Black)
3 balls of second colour (Red)
1 ball of third colour (White)
1 ball of fourth colour (Grey) for embroidery
1 pair each of 3mm/US size 3 and 6mm/US size 10 knitting needles
Approximately 5m/5½yd of silver sequin trim

SIZE

To fit 86-102cm/34-40in bust. See diagram for finished

Vivienne Bannister

Vivienne Bannister is a comparative newcomer to the field of fashion knitting, but set to do well in her new career. After studying art, she spent eleven years teaching, but never lost her enthusiasm for designing knits, supplying her friends with garments on private commissions. A craft potter friend suggested she showed at fairs nearby (she lives near the beautiful English South Coast resort, Hastings). The response was startling, and gave Vivienne the confidence to set up her own business. For the past two years her beautiful mohairs and tweedy thick wool knits have sold under the Outré label to exclusive stores in America and in England like The London Store at The Ritz; Ice, Los Angeles; Review of London in Nashville, Tennessee, not to mention Saks, Fifth Avenue. These bold designs are typical of her confident, witty style.

measurements and position of sequin trim.

TENSION/GAUGE

16 sts and 20 rows to 10cm/4in over st st on 6mm/US size 10 needles.

Note Use a separate length of yarn for each section and twist yarns together on wrong side of work on every row to avoid a hole. Read odd numbered rows from right to left and even numbered rows from left to right.

ABBREVIATIONS

See page 11.

BACK

With smaller needles and M, cast on 90 sts and work 16 rows in K1, P1 rib, working in patt from chart. Change to larger needles: keeping patt correct as set and beg with a K row, cont in st st until 115 rows of chart are complete. Cont in M only until back measures 60cm/23½in from beg, ending with a P row.

Shape shoulders
Cast/bind off 25 sts at beg of next 2 rows. Leave rem 40 sts on a holder for neckband.

FRONT

Work as back until front is 18 rows less than back to shoulders.

Shape neck
Keeping patt correct:
Next row K 40, turn and leave rem sts on a spare needle.
Cast/bind off 2 sts at beg of next and foll 3 alternate rows. Dec one st at neck edge on next 4 rows. Work one row without shaping. Dec one st at beg of next and every foll alternate row until 25 sts rem. Cast/bind off.
Return to sts on spare needle; with RS facing, sl first 10 sts on to a holder for neckband, rejoin M to neck edge, cast/bind off 2 sts and patt to end. Cont to match first side, reversing shaping.

SLEEVES

With smaller needles and M, cast on 40 sts and work 10 rows in K1, P1 rib, working in patt from chart. change to larger needles; keeping patt correct as set and beg with a K row, cont in st st working inc sts as shown on chart. 80 sts. When 76 rows of chart are complete, cast/bind off *loosely*.

NECKBAND

Join left shoulder seam.

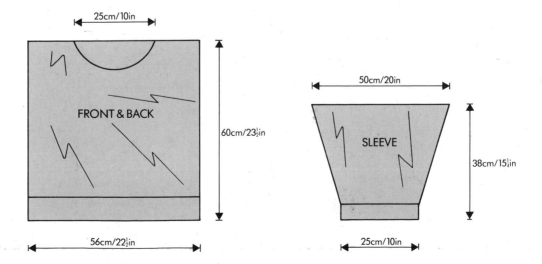

With smaller needles, M and RS facing, K back neck sts from holder, pick up and K 18 sts evenly down left front neck, K front neck sts from holder then pick up and K 18 sts evenly up right front neck. 86 sts.
Work 5 rows in K1, P1 rib, then cast/bind off *loosely* using larger needles.

FINISHING

Do not press.
Join right shoulder and neckband seam. Sew in sleeves, with centre of sleeve to shoulder seam. Using 2 strands of C tog and in chain st, work embroidery following diagram. Sew sequin trim on top of chain stitch, using couching stitch to catch down the strand of sequins. Join side and sleeve seams.

KEY TO CHART
M = □ = Black
· = Red
x = White

25cm/10in

FRONT & BACK

60cm/23½in

56cm/22½in

50cm/20in

SLEEVE

38cm/15¼in

25cm/10in

Beatrice Hympendahl

Beatrice Hympendahl likes to say she designs for 'demanding' women – perhaps because she works to high standards herself, and thrives under pressure. The daughter of a Kiel fur merchant, she has a strong background in the world of fashion. She was an apprentice in a couture business in Germany, next at the Ecole de Beaux Arts in Paris, and then studied at a fashion school in Frankfurt for a trade degree. She launched a shop in 1965, but marriage and children soon interrupted her career. She is quite frank that her breakthrough in fashion has occurred since her divorce and re-launch in 1978 with her own retail collection of textile fashions and knits.

Beatrice has her own shop in Düsseldorf but sells widely in West Germany through top stores like the Shewitt chain. Now she is expanding internationally with her own range featured in Harrods' Designer Collections.

Her clothes are strong in line with minimum frills or decorations, and she believes women like to buy her clothes to last for several years, adding different items each season. Knits interest her 'because fashion is turning to softer colours, a more natural look. The real art lies in minimizing, rather than adding.' This glittery sweater exemplifies her taste for confident, striking looks.

Vicky Mora

Vicky Mora is the most truly international individual among the designers featured here. Born in Austria, he designs and manufactures all his knitwear in Italy; he has homes in Austria, Florida and Italy, and spends two-thirds of the year travelling to fashion fairs worldwide. His knits are very luxurious and glamorous – the kind favoured in Aspen Colorado, Palm Springs, Rome or Dubai. The shared ingredient in all these markets is a love of classic materials, silk, cashmere, mohair, the finest glittering threads and trimmings.

Vicky Mora has been growing in reputation since he started fashion designing in 1974. After two years he decided to focus on luxury knits rather than the mass market, and now his designs are bought by the top Parisian couturiers. Soon he will expand into his own ready-to-wear. A handsome, approachable man, Vicky carefully selected one of his simpler designs that hand-knitters could achieve effectively rather than struggling with his satin appliqué or gemstone embroidery, which requires a high degree of technical skill. It is simply elegant, and very flattering.

· ZIG-ZAG SWEATER ·

Vicky Mora's pretty angora sweater is easy to make. Use different balls of yarn to avoid stranding across the back.

Bouton D'Or's *Angora and Wool Mix* was used for this pattern as it is available in many colours. Three shades of pink or black, grey and white are also pretty. If you substitute with other angora yarns, be sure to check the tension.

MATERIALS

7×20g/¾oz balls of Bouton D'Or's *70% Angora, 30% wool* in first colour A (Dark)
5 balls in second colour B (Medium)
4 balls in third colour C (Light)
1 pair each of 2¾mm/US size 2 and 3mm/US size 3 knitting needles.

SIZE

To fit 86-97cm/34-38in bust. See diagram for finished measurements.

TENSION/GAUGE

28 sts and 31 rows to 10cm/4in over st st in 3mm/US size 3 needles.

Note Use a separate length of yarn for each section and twist yarns together on every row to avoid a hole. Read odd numbered rows K from right to left and even numbered rows P from left to right.

ABBREVIATIONS

See page 11.

BACK AND FRONT (alike)

With smaller needles and A, cast on 143 sts.

1st row (RS) K1, [P1, K1] to end.
2nd row P1, [K1, P1] to end.
Rep last 2 rows 12 times more, inc one st in centre of last row. 144 sts. Change to larger needles. Beg with a K row and working in st st throughout, cont in patt from chart until 102 rows in all have been worked from top of rib.

Shape armholes

Keeping patt correct, cast/bind off 8 sts at beg of next 4 rows, then 2 sts at beg of next 16 rows. 80 sts. Cont without shaping until 2 complete patts have been worked. Work 30 rows in C.

Shape shoulders and neck

Cast/bind off 14 sts at beg of next 2 rows. Work 10 rows on rem 52 sts. Cast/bind off.

SLEEVES

With smaller needles and A, cast on 65 sts and work 26 rows in rib as on body, inc one st in centre of last row. 66 sts.
Change to larger needles.
1st row K9A, [K24 sts of first row of chart] twice, K9A.
This positions patt. Beg with a P row and working in st st, cont from chart as set, inc one st at each end of the 2nd and every foll alternate row until there are 112 sts, then every foll 4th row until there are 144 sts. Cont without shaping until sleeve measures 45cm/17¾in from beg, ending with a P row.

Shape top

Keeping patt correct, cast/bind off 8 sts at beg of next 4 rows. 112 sts. Cont without shaping until 2 complete patts have been worked. Work 8 rows in C. Dec one st at each end of the next 20 rows. Cast/bind off rem 72 sts.

FINISHING

Press according to instructions on yarn label. Join shoulder seams. Fold neck facing to inside and sew in place. Sew in sleeves, gathering tops to fit. Join side and sleeve seams. Press seams.

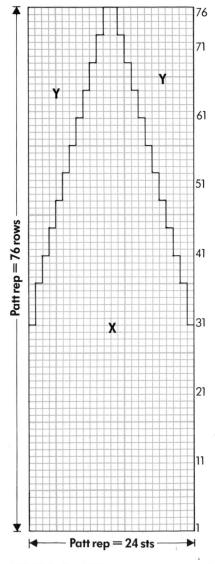

Patt rep = 76 rows

Patt rep = 24 sts

KEY TO CHART
On rows 1-76, X = A and Y = B
On rows 77-152, X = B and Y = C

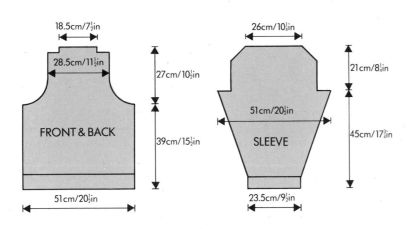

18.5cm/7½in

28.5cm/11½in

27cm/10½in

FRONT & BACK

39cm/15½in

51cm/20½in

26cm/10¼in

21cm/8¼in

51cm/20½in

SLEEVE

45cm/17¾in

23.5cm/9½in

BEATRICE HYMPENDAHL

◆ BRONZE MOTIF SWEATER ◆

Beatrice Hympendahl's design is a stunner that could be worn all day, all evening, with other jackets or by itself as it is versatile and classic in shape. The same idea could be reinterpreted in a range of fine weight glittery yarns – or you can use other glittery and plain yarns together, as here, with Bouton D'Or's *Zephyr* and *Etoile*.

See Yarn Suppliers for details of mail ordering on page 123.

MATERIALS

6×40g/1½oz balls of Bouton D'Or's *Zephyr* in main colour (Bistre)
11×20g/¾oz balls of Bouton D'Or's *Etoile* in first contrasting colour (Antelope)
2×20g/¾oz balls of Bouton D'Or's *Etoile* in second contrasting colour (Mordore)
1 pair each of 2¾mm/US size 2 and 3¼mm/US size 3 knitting needles
Set of four 2¾mm/US size 3 double pointed needles
2 shoulder pads

SIZE

To fit 86-97cm/34-38in bust. See diagram for finished measurements.

TENSION/GAUGE

28 sts and 34 rows to 10cm/4in over st st on 3¼/US size 3 needles.

Note Use a separate length of yarn for each section and twist yarns together on every row to avoid a hole. Read odd numbered rows K from right to left and even numbered rows P from left to right. Two strands of yarn are used together throughout. (You can Swiss darn the outer stitches, if preferred, see page 118.)

ABBREVIATIONS

M – one strand each of main yarn and first contrasting yarn used together.
C – two strands of second contrasting yarn used together. Also see page 11.

FRONT

With smaller needles and M, cast on 154 sts.
1st row (RS) K2, [P2, K2] to end.
2nd row P2, [K2, P2] to end.
Rep last 2 rows until rib measures 16cm/6¼in from beg, ending with a 2nd row and inc 3 sts evenly across the last row. 157 sts. ******
Change to larger needles. Beg with a K row, cont in st st inc one st at each end of the 7th and every foll 8th row until there are 167 sts. Work 5 rows without shaping. Inc one st at each end of next row. 169 sts. Work 5 rows without shaping.
Next row With M, inc in first st, K 77M, 1C, 11M, 1C, with M, K to last st, inc in last st. 171 sts.
Next row P 79M, 1C, 11M, 1C, 79M.
This sets position of patt.
Beg with row 3 and working throughout in st st, cont in patt from chart, still inc at each end of every 6th row as set, until there are 177 sts. Cont without shaping until front measures 38cm/15in from beg, ending with a P row.

KEY TO CHART
x = C

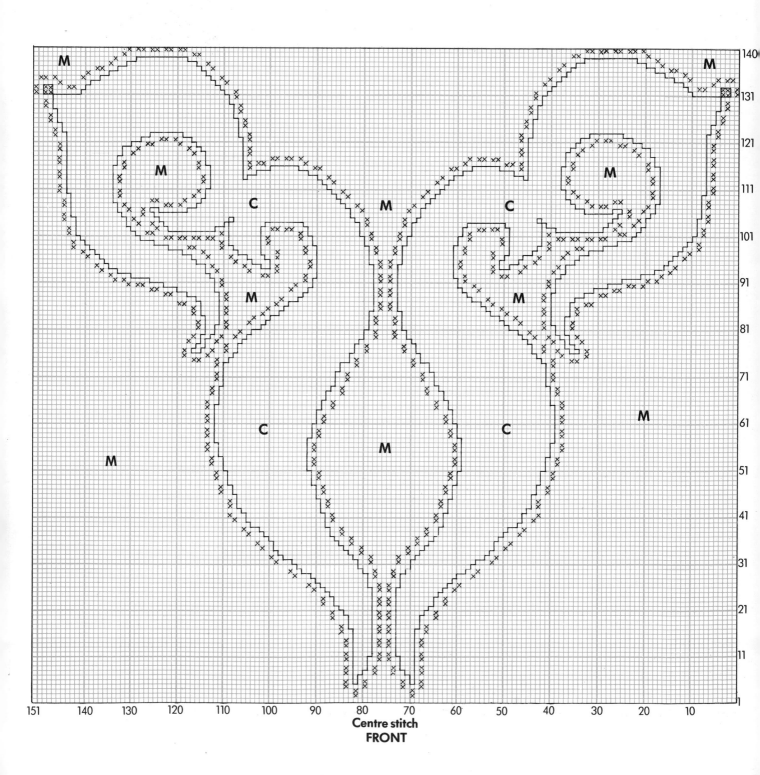

Centre stitch
FRONT

Shape armholes

Keeping patt correct, cast/bind off 4 sts at beg of next 2 rows, then 2 sts at beg of next 2 rows. Dec one st at each end of next and every foll alternate row until 151 sts rem. Cont without shaping until 116 rows in all have been worked from chart.

Shape neck

Next row Patt 63, turn and leave rem sts on a spare needle.
Cast/bind off 3 sts at beg of next and foll alternate row, then 2 sts at beg of foll 2 alternate rows. Dec one st at end of next and every foll alternate row until 45 sts rem and 139 rows of chart are complete. Cont in M only; work one row without shaping.

Shape shoulder

Cast/bind off 9 sts at beg of next and foll 3 alternate rows. Work one row without shaping, then cast/bind off rem 9 sts.
Return to sts on spare needle; with RS facing, sl first 25 sts on to a holder for neckband, rejoin M to neck edge, then cast/bind off 3 sts and patt to end. Cont to match first side, reversing all shaping.

BACK

Work as given for front to **.
Change to larger needles. Beg with a K row, cont in st st inc one st at each end of the 7th and every foll 8th row until there are 167 sts, then every foll 6th row until there are 177 sts. Cont without shaping until back measures same as front to armholes, ending with a P row.

Shape armholes

Cast/bind off 4 sts at beg of next 2 rows, then 2 sts at beg of next 2 rows. Dec one st at each end of next and every foll alternate row until 151 sts rem. Cont without shaping until armholes are 10 rows less than on front.

Shape neck

Next row K63, turn and leave rem

sts on a spare needle.
Cast/bind off 4 sts at beg of next and foll 2 alternate rows, then 3 sts at beg of foll 2 alternate rows. 45 sts.

Shape shoulder

Cast/bind off 9 sts at beg of next and foll 3 alternate rows. Work one row without shaping, then cast off rem 9 sts.
Return to sts on spare needle; with RS facing, sl first 25 sts on to a holder for neckband, rejoin M to neck edge, cast/bind off 4 sts and K to end. Cont to match first side, reversing all shaping.

SLEEVES

With smaller needles and M, cast on 114 sts and work 3cm/1¼in in rib as on front, ending with a 2nd row and inc 2 sts evenly across the last row. 116 sts.
Change to larger needles. Beg with a K row, cont in st st, inc one st at each end of the 3rd and every foll alternate row until there are 154 sts. Cont without shaping until sleeve measures 16cm/6¼in from beg, ending with a P row.

Shape top

Cast/bind off 4 sts at beg of next 2 rows, then 2 sts at beg of next 2 rows. Dec one st at each end of next and every foll alternate row until 114 sts rem, then at each end of every row until 74 sts rem. Cast/bind off 5 sts at beg of next 10 rows. Cast/bind off rem 24 sts.

NECKBAND

Join shoulder seams.
With set of four double pointed needles, M and RS facing, pick up and K 26 sts evenly down left front neck, K front neck sts from holder, pick up and K 26 sts evenly up right front neck and 15 sts down right back neck, K back neck sts from holder, then pick up and K 15 sts evenly up left back neck. 132 sts.
Work 6cm/2½in in rounds of K2, P2 rib. Cast/bind off *loosely* in rib.

FINISHING

Press pieces lightly as instructed on yarn label, avoiding ribbing. Sew in sleeves. Join side and sleeve seams. Fold neckband in half to inside and sew in place. Press seams. Sew in shoulder pads.

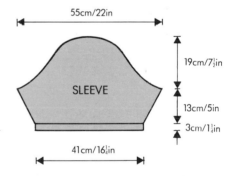

55cm/22in

19cm/7½in

SLEEVE

13cm/5in

3cm/1¼in

41cm/16¼in

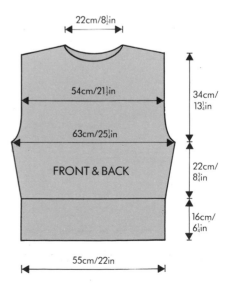

22cm/8½in

54cm/21½in

63cm/25¼in

34cm/13¼in

FRONT & BACK

22cm/8¼in

16cm/6¼in

55cm/22in

La Squadra

La Squadra Sisters System stands for the work of three
chic and beautiful French women, the Ottogruc sisters –
Gaetane, the eldest and Charlotte and Michelle, who
are twins. They are based in Monaco, and work entirely
together; designing and managing the company
between them. (La Squadra is 'team' in Italian.) 'We
virtually live together too!' Gaetane explained,
describing the creative process as one where an idea
forms and each sister develops it in her own way, for
different garments – leather work, machine-knits or
hand-knit fashion.
La Squadra have been in the forefront of French fashion
for over a decade. They have establishments in New
York and Paris as well as the South of France, but sell all
over the world. They are noted for the complex,
sophisticated styles they produce: beautifully stitched
leather jackets, two-piece knit suits and dresses that
blend many subtle colours in abstract patterns, and
hand-knits enriched with embroidery.

'FLEUR' LACE SWEATER

La Squadra's appliquéd sweater gives knitting a new look – the trend is towards smoother yarns, with more decorative detail, in patches or applied stitching. Hayfield's *Lugano* is available in both plain and 'mixer' shades, ideal for matching with a few beautiful fabric pieces, picking out colours that complement each other. Stitch the appliqué pieces to the knitting only after it has been blocked to avoid distortion in the shape.

MATERIALS

8×50g/1¾oz balls of Hayfield's *Lugano*
1 pair each of 4mm/US size 6 and 7½mm/US size 11 knitting needles
Fabric remnants for appliqué
Matching thread

SIZE

To fit 86-97cm/34-38in bust.
See diagram for finished measurements.

TENSION/GAUGE

15 sts and 18 rows to 10cm/4in over st st on 7½mm/US size 11 needles.

ABBREVIATIONS

yfwd/yarn forward – yarn to front of work between needles, then to back of work over right hand needle to form a new loop.
See also page 11.

LACE PANEL (13 sts)

1st row yfwd, K2tog, K7, K2tog, yfwd, K2.
2nd and every foll alternate row P to end.

3rd row K1, yfwd, K2tog, K5, K2tog, yfwd, K3.
5th row K2, yfwd, K2tog, K3, K2tog, yfwd, K4.
7th row K3, yfwd, K2tog, K1, K2tog, yfwd, K5.
9th row K5, K2tog, yfwd, K6.
11th row K4, K2tog, yfwd, K7.
13th row K3, K2tog, yfwd, K8.
15th row K2, K2tog, yfwd, K9.
17th row K2, yfwd, K2tog, K7, K2tog, yfwd.
19th row K3, yfwd, K2tog, K5, K2tog, yfwd, K1.
21st row K4, yfwd, K2tog, K3, K2tog, yfwd, K2.
23rd row K5, yfwd, K2tog, K1, K2tog, yfwd, K3.
25th row K6, yfwd, K2tog, K5.
27th row K7, yfwd, K2tog, K4.
29th row K8, yfwd, K2tog, K3.
31st row K9, yfwd, K2tog, K2.
32nd row As 2nd row.
These 32 rows form the rep of panel.

FRONT

With smaller needles, cast on 82 sts.
1st row (RS) K2, [P2, K2] to end.
2nd row P2, [K2, P2] to end.
Rep the last 2 rows 19 times more, inc one st in centre of last row. 83 sts.
Change to larger needles and cont in patt as foll: *
1st row K35, patt 13 sts as first row of panel, K to end.
2nd row P35, patt 13 sts as 2nd row of panel, P to end.
This sets position of patt, keeping panel sts correct and remaining sts in st st throughout, cont until 82 rows in all have been worked from top of rib.

Shape neck
Next row Patt 36, turn and leave rem sts on a spare needle.

Cast/bind off 2 sts at beg of next and foll 4 alternate rows. Work 3 rows without shaping.
Cast/bind off.
Return to sts on spare needle; with RS facing, sl first 11 sts on to a holder for neckband, rejoin yarn to neck edge, cast/bind off 2 sts and K to end. Cont to match first side, reversing shaping.

BACK

Work as given for front to *.
1st row K9, [patt 13 sts as first row of panel, K13] twice, patt 13 sts as first row of panel, K to end.
2nd row P9, [patt 13 sts as 2nd row of panel, P13] twice, patt 13 sts as 2nd row of panel, P to end.
This sets position of patt, keeping panel sts correct and remaining sts in st st throughout, cont until 96 rows in all have been worked from top of rib.

Shape shoulders
Cast/bind off 26 sts at beg of next 2 rows. Leave rem 31 sts on a holder for neckband.

SLEEVES

With smaller needles, cast on 42 sts and work 30 rows in rib as on front, inc 2 sts evenly across the last row. 44 sts.
Change to larger needles and cont in patt as foll:
1st row K2, patt 13 sts as first row of panel, K14, patt 13 sts as first row of panel, K to end.
2nd row P2, patt 13 sts as 2nd row of panel, P14, patt 13 sts as 2nd row of panel, P to end.
This sets position of patt, keeping panel sts correct and remaining sts in st st throughout, inc one st at each end of the next and every foll 3rd row until there are 84 sts. Cont

without shaping until sleeve measures 48cm/19in from beg, ending with a P row. Cast/bind off *loosely*.

NECKBAND

Join left shoulder seam.
With smaller needles and RS facing, K back neck sts from holder inc 6 sts evenly across them, pick up and K 20 sts evenly down left front neck, K front neck sts from holder inc 2 sts evenly across them, then pick up and K 20 sts evenly up right front neck. 90 sts.
Work 20 rows in rib as on front.
Cast/bind off *loosely* in rib.

FINISHING

Do not press. Join right shoulder and neckband seam. Sew in sleeves, with centre of sleeve to shoulder seam. Join side and sleeve seams. Fold neckband in half to inside and sew in place.

APPLIQUÉ

Cut appliqué pieces as desired or following diagram. Machine edge with zigzag stitch.
Pin pieces in place and sew carefully around edges.

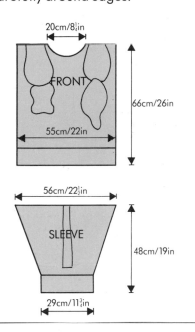

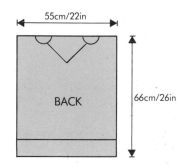

· MAEYR ·

La Squadra's design, *Maeyr*, is a brilliantly adaptable sweater, neatly shaped at the rib and the neckline to sit well. Sirdar's *Nocturne* is available in a range of soft neutral tones, but other bulky weight mohairs could be used. *Nocturne* has a fine core and a great deal of bulk, and is knitted to a loose tension in this pattern; try not to substitute with too thick a mohair, for a similar result.

MATERIALS

10×25g/1oz balls of Sirdar's *Nocturne* in first colour A (Ecru)
6 balls in second colour B (Beige)

One spool of fine glitter tape such as Twilley's *Goldfingering* for rib, and oddments for embroidery
Oddments in each of approximately 6 bulky weight mohair colours for embroidery (to match glitter tape)
1 pair each of 5mm/US size 8 and 7mm/US size 10½ knitting needles
1 darning needle, blunt-ended

SIZE

To fit 86(pl:97)cm/34(36:38)in bust.
See diagram for finished measurements.

TENSION/GAUGE

15 sts and 17 rows to 10cm/4in over st st on 7mm/US size 10½ needles.

Note Use a separate length of yarn for each section and twist yarns together on every row to avoid a hole. Read odd numbered rows K from right to left and even numbered rows P from left to right. See Technical Section (page 118) for further information on block knitting.

ABBREVIATIONS

See page 11.

FRONT

With smaller needles and one strand each of A and glitter tape tog, cast on 72(76:80)sts and work 10 rows in g st. Break off glitter tape. Change to larger needles and K one row, inc 8 sts evenly across the row. 80(84:88)sts. *
Beg with P row, work 5 rows st st. Beg with row 7, cont in patt from chart until 84(86:90) rows in all have been worked in st st.

Shape neck
Next row Patt 36(37:38), turn and leave rem sts on a spare needle. Cast/bind off 3 sts at beg of next

and foll 2 alternate rows, 2 sts at beg of foll 2 alternate rows, then one st at beg of foll alternate row. Work 4 rows without shaping. Cast/bind off.
Return to sts on spare needle; with RS facing, sl first 8(10:12)sts on to a holder for neckband, rejoin B to neck edge, cast/bind off 3 sts and patt to end. Cont to match first side, reversing shaping.

BACK

Work as given for front to *.
Beg with a P row, cont in st st until back measures the same as front to shoulders, ending with a P row.

Shape shoulders
Cast/bind off 22(23:24) sts at beg of next 2 rows. Leave rem 36(38:40)sts on a holder for neckband.

FIRST SLEEVE

With smaller needles and one strand each of A and glitter tape tog, cast on 32(36:40)sts and work 10 rows in g st. Break off glitter tape. Change to larger needles and K one row inc 6 sts evenly across the row. 38(42:46)sts.
Beg with a P row, cont in st st, inc one st at each end of the 2nd and every foll 3rd row until there are

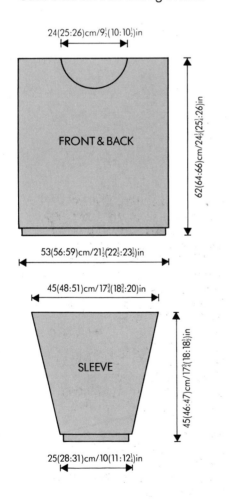

24(25:26)cm/9½(10:10½)in

FRONT & BACK

62(64:66)cm/24½(25½:26)in

53(56:59)cm/21½(22½:23½)in

45(48:51)cm/17¾(18¾:20)in

SLEEVE

45(46:47)cm/17¾(18:18½)in

25(28:31)cm/10(11:12¼)in

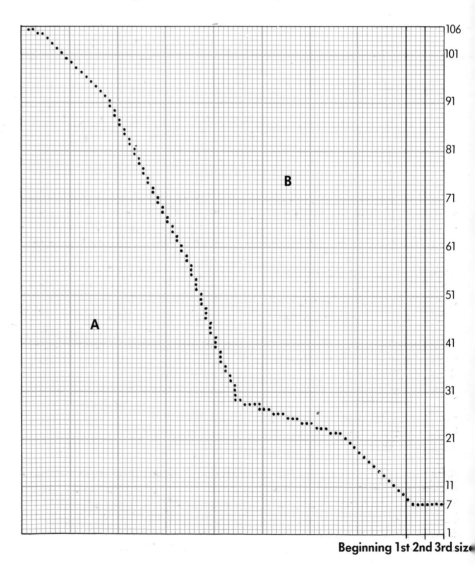

B

A

106
101
91
81
71
61
51
41
31
21
11
7
1

Beginning 1st 2nd 3rd size

68(72:76)sts. Cont without shaping until sleeve measures 45(46:47)cm/17¾(18:18½)in from beg, ending with a P row. Cast/bind off *loosely*.

SECOND SLEEVE

Work as given for first sleeve, *but* using B instead of A.

NECKBAND

Join left shoulder seam. With smaller needles, one strand each of A and glitter tape tog and RS facing, K back neck sts from holder, pick up and K 11 sts evenly down left front neck, K front neck sts from holder, then pick up and K 11 sts evenly up right front neck. 66(70:74)sts.
Work 8 rows in g st. Cast/bind off *loosely*.

FINISHING

Do not press. Join right shoulder and neckband seam. Sew in sleeves, with centre of sleeve to shoulder seam. Join side and sleeve seams. Work cross stitch embroidery (see page 121): and use various colours of mohair, mixed with glitter tape to match attractively.

GLYNIS ROBINS

· Aran Sweater ·

Glynis Robins's designs are subtle variations on traditional Irish patterns, and not at all difficult for an average knitter to make. This design was knitted in Rowan's *Spun Tweed*, but any medium weight yarn could be tried out for this pattern. Rowan's *Designer DK Cotton* is good for summer wear.

MATERIALS

8×100g/3½oz hanks of Rowan's *Spun Tweed*
1 pair each of 3¼mm/US size 3 and 3¾mm/US size 5 and 4½mm/US size 7 knitting needles
1 cable needle

SIZES

To fit 86(91:97)cm/34(36:38)in bust.
See diagram for finished measurements.

TENSION/GAUGE

21 sts and 24 rows to 10cm/4in over patt on 4½mm/US size 7 needles.

ABBREVIATIONS

MB – [K1, K1 tbl] twice into next st, turn, P4, turn, K4, sl 2nd, 3rd and 4th sts over first st and off needle.
C4B – sl next 2 sts to cable needle to back of work, K2, then K2 from cable needle.
C4F – sl next 2 sts to cable needle to front of work, K2, then K2 from cable needle.
Also see page 11.

BACK

With 3¾mm/US size 5 needles, cast on 97(101:105)sts.
1st row (RS) K1 tbl, [P1, K1 tbl] to end.
2nd row P1, [K1 tbl, P1] to end.
Rep the last 2 rows until rib measures 7cm/2¾in from beg, ending with a 2nd row and inc 13 sts evenly across the last row. 110(114:118)sts. Change to 4½mm/US size 7 needles and cont in patt as foll:
1st row K 50(52:54), P1, K3, P1, K4, P1, [P1, K1] to end.
2nd row [K1, P1] 25(26:27) times, K1, P4, K1, P3, K1, P to end.
3rd row K 50(52:54), P1, K3, P1, C4F, P1, [K1, P1] to end.
4th row [P1, K1] 25(26:27) times, K1, P4, K1, P3, K1, P to end.
5th row As first row.
6th row As 2nd row.
7th row K 50(52:54), P1, K1, MB, K1, P1, C4B, P1, [K1, P1] to end.
8th row [P1, K1] 25(26:27) times, K1, P4, K1, P3, K to end.
These 8 rows form the rep of patt. Cont as set until back measures 37cm/14½in from beg, ending with a WS row.

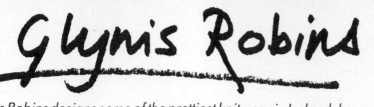

Glynis Robins

Glynis Robins designs some of the prettiest knitwear in Ireland; her work is shown in the Galeria of Fashion in St. Stephen's Green, but sells all over the world. She trained in Dublin and then at New York's Fashion Institute of Technology; on her return to Ireland she was commissioned to produce designs for Kenzo Takada in Paris. Now her own business is expanding rapidly from her workshop in the village of Dalkey, a favourite haunt of craftsmen and artists on Dublin Bay. Recently she has added a range of beautifully stitched linen shift-shaped dresses to her collections. Her hand-knits have a femininity and a freshness about them, combining Irish traditional motifs with soft colourings and simple, flattering shapes.

Shape armholes

Keeping patt correct, cast/bind off 4 sts at beg of next 2 rows. 102(106:110)sts.
Cont without shaping until armholes measure 30cm/11¾in, ending with a WS row.

Shape shoulders

Cast/bind off 32(34:36)sts at beg of next 2 rows. Leave rem 38 sts on a holder for neckband.

FRONT

Work as given for back until armholes measure 22cm/8½in, ending with a WS row.

Shape neck

Next row Patt 45(47:49), turn and leave rem sts on a spare needle. Cast/bind off 3 sts at beg of next and foll alternate row, 2 sts at beg of foll 2 alternate rows, then one st at beg of foll 3 alternate rows. 32(34:36)sts.
Cont without shaping until armholes measure the same as on back, ending with a WS row. Cast/bind off.
Return to sts on spare needle: with RS facing, sl first 12 sts on to a holder for neckband, rejoin yarn to neck edge, cast/bind off 3 sts, patt to end. Cont to match first side, reversing shaping, and ending with 32(34:36) sts to cast/bind off.

SLEEVES

With 3¾mm/US size 5 needles, cast on 45 sts and work 7cm/2¾in in rib as on back, ending with a 2nd row and inc one st in centre of last row. 46 sts.
Change to 4½mm/US size 7 needles and cont in patt as foll:
1st row K18, P1, K3, P1, K4, P1, [P1, K1] to end.
2nd row [K1, P1] 9 times, K1, P4, K1, P3, K1, P to end.
This sets position of patt. Cont in patt to match back, inc one st at each end of the next and every foll 4th row until there are 64 sts, then every foll alternate row, working inc sts into patt until there are 126 sts. Cont without shaping until sleeve measures 50cm/19½in from beg, ending with a WS row. Cast/bind off *loosely*.

NECKBAND

Join left shoulder seam.
With 3¾mm/US size 5 needles and RS facing, K back neck sts from holder, pick up and K 23 sts evenly down left front neck, K front neck sts from holder, then pick up and K 24 sts evenly up right front neck. 97 sts.
Beg with a 2nd row, work 3 rows in rib as on back. Change to 3¼mm/US size 3 needles. Work 2 more rows, then cast/bind off *loosely* in rib.

FINISHING

Do not press.
Join right shoulder and neckband seam.
Sew in sleeves. Join side and sleeve seams.

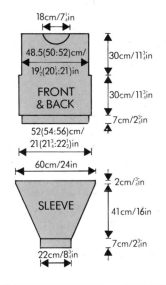

18cm/7¼in
48.5(50:52)cm/
19½(20¼:21)in
FRONT & BACK
30cm/11¾in
30cm/11¾in
7cm/2¾in
52(54:56)cm/
21(21¾:22½)in

60cm/24in
2cm/¾in
SLEEVE
41cm/16in
7cm/2¾in
22cm/8¾in

◆ *Basket Stitch Sweater* ◆

For the less experienced knitter, this Glynis Robins sweater is ideal. Once the basket stitch has been mastered, it is repeated on a smaller scale, and the rest of the design is knitted in a simple rib.

MATERIALS

9 × 100g/3½oz hanks of Rowan's *Spun Tweed*
1 pair each of 3¾mm/US size 5 and 4½mm/US size 7 knitting needles.

SIZES

To fit 86(91:97:102)cm/ 34(36:38:40)in bust.
See diagram for finished measurements.

TENSION/GAUGE

18 sts and 24 rows to 10cm/4in over patt on 4½mm/US size 7 needles.

ABBREVIATIONS

See page 11.

BACK

With smaller needles, cast on 78(86:94:102)sts.
1st row (RS) K2 tbl, [P2, K2 tbl] to end.
2nd row P2, [K2 tbl, P2] to end.
Rep the last 2 rows until rib measures 9cm/3½in from beg, ending with a 2nd row and inc 6 sts evenly across the last row. 84(92:100:108)sts.
Change to larger needles and cont in patt as foll:
1st row K4, [P4, K4] to end.
2nd row P4, [K4, P4] to end.
Rep the last 2 rows once more.
5th row As 2nd row.
6th row As first row.
Rep the last 2 rows once more.
These 8 rows form the rep of patt 1.
Cont until back measures approximately 28cm/11in from beg, ending with a 4th or 8th patt row.
Cont in patt 2 as foll:
1st row K2, [P8, K8] to last 2(10:2:10)sts, P 2(8:2:8), K 0(2:0:2).
2nd row P2, [K8, P8] to last 2(10:2:10)sts, K 2(8:2:8), P 0(2:0:2).
Rep the last 2 rows 3 times more.
9th row As 2nd row.
10th row As first row.
Rep the last 2 rows 3 times more.
These 16 rows form the rep of patt 2.
Cont until back measures approximately 46cm/18in from beg, ending with an 8th or 16th patt row.
Cont in patt 3 as foll:
1st row K4 tbl, [P4, K4 tbl] to end.
2nd row P4, [K4 tbl, P4] to end.
Rep the last 2 rows until back measures 61cm/24in from beg, ending with a WS row.

Shape shoulders
Cast/bind off 29(33:37:41)sts at beg of next 2 rows.
Leave rem 26 sts on a holder for collar.

FRONT

Work as given for back until front measures 48cm/18¾in from beg, ending with a RS row.

Divide for front opening
Next row Patt 46(50:54:58), turn and leave rem sts on a spare needle.
Cont without shaping until front measures 54cm/21¼ from beg, ending with a WS row.

Shape neck
Cast/bind off 7 sts at beg of next row, 3 sts at beg of foll 2 alternate rows, 2 sts at beg of foll alternate row, then one st at beg of foll 2 alternate rows. 29(33:37:41)sts.
Cont without shaping until front measures the same as back to shoulders, ending with a RS row.
Cast/bind off.
Return to sts on spare needle: with WS facing, rejoin yarn to neck edge, cast on 8 sts and patt to end.
Cont to match first side, reversing shaping.

SLEEVES

With smaller needles, cast on 42 sts and work 9cm/3½in in rib as on back, ending with a 2nd row and inc 10 sts evenly across the last row. 52 sts.
Change to larger needles. Cont in patt as on first size of back, inc one st at each end of the 3rd and every foll alternate row, working inc sts into patt until there are 142 sts, ending with a WS row. Cast/bind off *loosely*.

COLLAR

Join shoulder seams.
With smaller needles and RS facing, pick up and K 28 sts evenly up right front neck, K back neck sts from holder, inc 6 sts evenly across them, then pick up and K 28 sts evenly down left front neck. 88 sts.
Beg with a 2nd row, work 12cm/4¾in in rib as on back. Cast/bind off *loosely* in rib.

FINISHING

Do not press.
Sew in sleeves, with centre of sleeve to shoulder seam. Join side and sleeve seams. Sew cast on sts at centre front behind overlap.

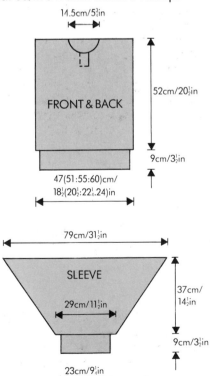

14.5cm/5⅝in

52cm/20½in

FRONT & BACK

9cm/3½in

47(51:55:60)cm/ 18½(20½:22¼:24)in

79cm/31½in

SLEEVE

37cm/ 14½in

29cm/11½in

9cm/3½in

23cm/9¼in

Louis Dell'Olio

The company for which Louis Dell'Olio is now Head Designer was started by Anne Klein in the 1950s, originally making superbly pretty clothes for smaller women – almost unheard of at the time. It has now grown into one of the biggest ready-to-wear companies in the USA. From 1974 when Anne Klein died, until 1985, Louis Dell'Olio worked in partnership with a fellow-student, Donna Karan, but now he alone supervises the large number of Anne Klein ranges and numerous license operations. Louis Dell'Olio won his first Coty Award in 1977, then a return award in 1981, and entered the Coty Hall of Fame in 1982.

All his designs, both in knits and fabric are quietly elegant and expensive looking, made of high quality textiles and yarns.

· BABY IGUANA ·

Joan Vass's *Baby Iguana* is aptly named after the little ridges of 'scales' that run up the rib pattern of the knitting. All Joan's designs are given personal names to make them as full of character and as individual as the people she hopes will enjoy them. Woolgatherers' *Flaminia* was chosen because of its flecky, tweedy look; the same design could work very well with other background yarns but remember that the lovely effect is achieved by the subtle graduating of colour in the angora 'scales'.

See pages 119-20 of the Technical Section for a reminder about crochet stitches.

MATERIALS

2×20g/1oz balls of Bouton D'Or's *70% Angora 30% Wool* in first colour A (Dark Pink)
1 ball in second colour B (Medium Pink)
1 ball in third colour C (Light Pink)
300/350/500g/10½/12/17½oz of Woolgatherers' *Flaminia* (D)
400/500/600g/14/17½/21oz of Woolgatherers' *Wool Aran Tweed* (E)
1 pair of 8mm/US size 11 knitting needles
4mm/US size 5 crochet hook

MEASUREMENTS

To fit 86(91:97)cm/34(36:38)in bust.
See diagram for finished measurements.

TENSION/GAUGE

11 sts and 20 rows to 10cm/4in over patt on 8mm/US size 11 needles.

Note One strand each of *Flaminia*, D, and *Aran Tweed*, E, are used together.

ABBREVIATIONS

dc/sc – double crochet/US single crochet
ch – chain
ss – slip stitch
Also see page 11.

BACK AND FRONT (worked in one piece)

With one strand each of D and E, cast on 49(51:55)sts.
1st row (RS) K 4(5:7), [P1, K4] to last 0(1:3)sts, K 0(1:3).
2nd row P 4(5:7), [K1, P4] to last 0(1:3)sts, P 0(1:3).
Rep last 2 rows until work measures 33(34:35)cm/13(13½:13¾)in from beg, ending with a WS row. Working inc sts into st st, inc one st at each end of next and foll two alternate rows. 55(57:61)sts.
Work one row without shaping.

Shape armholes
Keeping patt correct, dec one st at each end of next and every foll alternate row until 45(47:51)sts rem. Cont without shaping until work measures 46(48:50)cm/18(19:19¾)in from beg, ending with a WS row.

Shape front neck
Next row Patt 16(17:19), cast/bind off 13 sts, patt to end.
Cont on last set of sts only, work one row without shaping. Dec one st at beg of next and foll alternate row. 14(15:17)sts.
Cont without shaping until work measures 52(54:56)cm/20½(21¼:22)in from beg, ending with a WS row. **

Shape back neck
Cast on 3 sts at beg of next row, then 11 sts at beg of foll alternate row. Do not break off yarn, but leave these sts on a spare needle. Return to sts that were left; with WS facing, rejoin one strand each of D and E to neck edge and patt to end. Cont to match first side to **, reversing shaping.
Work one row without shaping.
Cast on 3 sts at beg of next row.
Work one row without shaping.
Return to sts on spare needle; with WS facing, patt to end across sts on spare needle, then patt to end across sts of left shoulder. 45(47:51)sts.
Cont without shaping until work measures 63(66:69)cm/24¾(26:27¼)in from beg, ending with a WS row. Inc one st at each end of next and every foll alternate row until there are 55(57:61)sts. Work one row without shaping.

Shape back
Dec one st at each end of next and every foll alternate row until 49(51:55)sts rem. Cont without shaping until back measures the same as front. Cast/bind off.

SLEEVES

With one strand each of D and E, cast on 28(30:32)sts.
1st row K 1(2:3), [P1, K4] to last 2(3:4)sts, P1, K 1(2:3).
2nd row P 1(2:3), [K1, P4] to last 2(3:4)sts, K1, P 1(2:3).
This sets position of patt. Work 8 rows without shaping. Inc one st at each end of next and every foll 12th row until there are 38(40:42)sts. Work 15(17:19) rows without shaping. Inc one st at each end of next and foll 2 alternate rows. 44(46:48)sts. Work one row without shaping.

Shape top
Dec one st at each end of next and every foll alternate row until 18 sts rem. Cast/bind off.

CROCHET DETAIL

Work into the 'ladder' formed by making P1 in patt.
Work 1dc/sc into first rung of ladder, 1dc/sc into 2nd, 1dc/sc into 3rd and 4th tog, 1dc/sc into 5th, 1dc/sc into 6th, *turn, 1ch, miss/skip first dc/sc, work 1dc/sc into next 5dc/sc, turn, 1ch, miss/skip first dc/sc, 1dc/sc into next 4dc/sc, turn, 1ch, miss/skip first dc/sc, 1dc/sc into next 3dc/sc, turn, 1ch, miss/skip first dc/sc, 1dc/sc into next 2dc/sc, sl st along to next rung of ladder. *
1dc/sc into 7th and 8th rungs tog, 1dc/sc into 9th, 1dc/sc into 10th, 1dc/sc into 11th and 12th tog, 1dc/sc into 13th, 1dc/sc into 14th.
Rep from * to *.
Cont as set, working every 3rd and 4th rung tog, up the full length of each ladder.
Starting at left side edge, work rows in graduating colours of angora yarn, as illustrated, or varying the colours as preferred. On sleeves, work up complete ladders only using A throughout.

FINISHING

Do not press. Join shoulder seams. Sew in sleeves. Join side and sleeve seams. With crochet hook, one strand of D and E and RS facing, work one round in dc/sc along lower edge on body and sleeves and around neck. Fasten off.

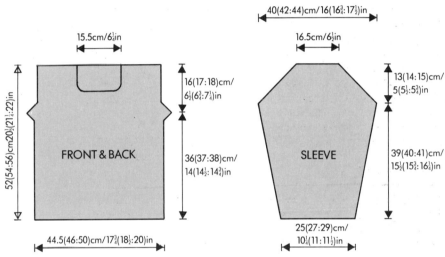

FRONT & BACK

SLEEVE

15.5cm/6¼in

52(54:56)cm/20½(21¼:22)in

44.5(46:50)cm/17¾(18½:20)in

16(17:18)cm/6½(6¾:7¼)in

36(37:38)cm/14(14½:14¾)in

40(42:44)cm/16(16¾:17½)in

16.5cm/6½in

13(14:15)cm/5(5½:5¾)in

39(40:41)cm/15½(15¾:16¼)in

25(27:29)cm/10¼(11:11½)in

LOUIS DELL'OLIO

·ROLL COLLAR ARAN·

Louis Dell'Olio's sweater is a great lesson in using traditional stitches and transforming them into high fashion. The cropped length is very flattering, and balanced beautifully by a generous collar and shoulder pads.
Woolgatherers' *Italian Pure Wool DK* was used as it is available in a wide variety of colours, but any DK wool that matches the tension/gauge given could be substituted.

MATERIALS

800g/28oz of pure double knitting wool
1 pair each of 3¾mm/US size 5 and 4½mm/US size 7 knitting needles
3¾mm/US size 5 circular needle 50cm/20in long
1 cable needle
2 shoulder pads

SIZE

To fit 86-97cm/34-38in bust. See diagrams for finished measurements.

TENSION/GAUGE

20 sts and 24 rows to 10cm/4in over patt on 4½mm/US size 7 needles.

ABBREVIATIONS

Inc 1 – work into front and back of next st.

MB – [K1, P1, K1] into front of next st.

C6B – sl next 3 sts to cable needle to back of work, K3, then K3 from cable needle.

C6F – sl next 3 sts to cable needle to front of work, K3, then K3 from cable needle.

C6BK – sl next 3 sts to cable needle to back of work, K3, then K1, P1, K1 from cable needle.

C6FK – sl next 3 sts to cable needle to front of work, K1, P1, K1, then K3 from cable needle.

C6BP – sl next 3 sts to cable needle to back of work, K3, then P1, K1, P1 from cable needle.

C6FP – sl next 3 sts to cable needle to front of work, P1, K1, P1, then K3 from cable needle.

Also see page 11.

BACK

With smaller needles, cast on 95 sts.

1st row (RS) K1, [P1, K1] to end.
2nd row P1, [K1, P1] to end.
Rep the last 2 rows until back measures 3cm/1¼in from beg, ending with a 2nd row. Change to larger needles and cont in patt as foll:

1st row Inc 1, P2, [K3, inc 1, K1, P10, inc 1, P12] 3 times, K3, inc 1, K1, P2, inc 1. 104 sts.
2nd row K4, *P6, K8, [MB, P3tog] twice, K8; rep from *twice more, P6, K4.
3rd row P4, [K6, P24] 3 times, K6, P4.
4th row Inc 1, K3, *P6, K8, [P3tog, MB] twice, K8; rep from *twice more, P6, K3, inc 1. 106 sts.
5th row P5, [K6, P24] 3 times, K6, P5.
6th row K5, *P6, K8, [MB, P3tog] twice, K8; rep from *twice more, P6, K5.
7th row Inc 1, P1, [K3, C6B, K3, P18] 3 times, K3, C6B, K3, P1, inc 1. 108 sts.

8th row K3, *P12, K5, [P3tog, MB] twice, K5; rep from *twice more, P12, K3.
9th row P3, [K12, P18] 3 times, K12, P3.
10th row Inc 1, K2, *P12, K5, [MB, P3tog] twice, K5; rep from *twice more, P12, K2, inc 1. 110 sts.
11th row P4, [K12, P18] 3 times, K12, P4.
12th row K4, *P12, K5, [P3tog, MB] twice, K5; rep from *twice more, P12, K4.
13th row Inc 1, *K3, C6BK, C6FP, K3, P2, K1, [P1, K1] 3 times, [P1, K1] into next st, P2; rep from *twice more, K3, C6BK, C6FP, K3 inc 1. 115 sts.
14th row K2, *P6 [P1, K1] 3 times, P6, K2, P9, K2; rep from *twice more, P6, [P1, K1] 3 times, P6, K2.
15th row P2, *K6, [K1, P1] 3 times, K6, P2, [K1, P1] 4 times, K1, P2; rep from *twice more, K6, [K1, P1] 3 times, K6, P2.
16th row Inc 1, K1, *P6, [P1, K1] 3 times, P6, K2, P9, K2; rep from *twice more, P6, [P1, K1] 3 times, P6, K1, inc 1. 117 sts.
17th row P3, *K6, [K1, P1] 3 times, K6, P2, [K1, P1] 4 times, K1, P2; rep from *twice more, K6, [K1, P1] 3 times, K6, P3.
18th row K3, *P6, [P1, K1] 3 times, P6, K2, P9, K2; rep from *twice more, P6, [P1, K1] 3 times, P6, K3.
19th row P3, *C6BP, [K1, P1] 3 times, C6FK, P2, [K1, P1] 4 times, K1, P2; rep from *twice more, C6BP, [K1, P1] 3 times, C6FK, P3.
20th row: K3, *P3 [K1, P1] 6 times, P3, K2, P9, K2; rep from *twice more, P3, [K1, P1] 6 times, P3, K3.
21st row P3, *K3, [P1, K1] 6 times, K3, P2, [K1, P1] 4 times, K1, P2; rep from *twice more, K3, [P1, K1] 6 times, K3, P3.
22nd row As 20th row.
23rd row As 21st row.
24th row As 20th row.
25th row P3, *C6F, [K1, P1] 3 times, C6B, P2, [K1, P1] 4 times, K1, P2; rep from *twice more, C6F, [K1, P1] 3 times, C6B, P3.
26th row As 18th row.
27th row As 17th row.

Rep the last 2 rows once more.
30th row As 18th row.
31st row P6, *C6F, C6B, P12, P2 tog, P5; rep from *twice more, C6F, C6B, P6. 114 sts.
32nd row K6, *P12, K5, [P3tog, MB] twice, K5; rep from *twice more, P12, K6.
33rd row P6, [K12, P18] 3 times, K12, P6.
34th row K6, *P12, K5, [MB, P3tog] twice, K5; rep from *twice more, P12, K6.
35th row As 33rd row.
36th row As 32nd row.
37th row P9, [C6B, P24] 3 times, C6B, P9.
38th row K9, *P6, K8, [MB, P3tog] twice, K8; rep from *twice more, P6, K9.
39th row P9, [K6, P24) 3 times, K6, P9.
40th row K9, *P6, K8, [P3tog, MB] twice, K8; rep from *twice more, P6, K9.
41st row As 39th row.
42nd row As 38th row.
43rd row P6, [K3, C6B, K3, P18] 3 times, K3, C6B, K3, P6.
44th row As 32nd row.
45th row As 33rd row.
46th row As 34th row.
47th row As 33rd row.
48th row As 32nd row.
49th row P3, *K3, C6BK, C6FP, K3, P2, K1, [P1, K1] 3 times, [P1, K1] into next st, P2; rep from *twice more, K3, C6BK, C6FP, K3, P3. 117 sts.
50th row K3, * P6 [P1, K1] 3 times, P6, K2, P9, K2; rep from *twice more, P6, [P1, K1] 3 times, P6, K3.
51st row P3, * K6 [K1, P1] 3 times, K6, P2, [K1, P1] 4 times, K1, P2; rep from *twice more, K6, [K1, P1] 3 times, K6, P3.
52nd row as 50th row.
Rows 17-52 form the rep of patt. **
Cont as set until work measures 45cm/17¾in from beg, ending with a WS row.

Shape shoulders and neck
Note Due to the nature of this patt the number of sts varies from row to row, when working all shaping

the number of sts quoted is the basic amount and does not include any sts made while working patt.
Next row Cast/bind off 7, patt 26 including st on needle after casting/binding off, cast/bind off 48, patt to end.
Cont on last set of sts only; cast/bind off 7 sts at beg of next and foll 2 alternate rows, AT THE SAME TIME, dec one st at neck edge on next 5 rows. Work one row without shaping, then cast/bind off rem 7 sts. Return to sts which were left; with WS facing, rejoin yarn to neck edge, dec one st and patt to end. Cont to match first side, reversing all shaping.

FRONT

Work as given for back to **.
Cont as set until front is 10 rows less than back to shoulders.

Shape neck
Next row Patt 43, cast/bind off 28, patt to end.
Cont on last set of sts only; dec one st at neck edge on next 10 rows.

Shape shoulders
Cast/bind off 7 sts at beg of next and foll 2 alternate rows, AT THE

SAME TIME, dec one st at neck edge on next 5 rows. Work one row without shaping, then cast/bind off rem 7 sts.
Return to sts which were left; with WS facing, rejoin yarn to neck edge dec one st and patt to end. Cont to match first side, reversing all shaping.

SLEEVES

With smaller needles, cast on 39 sts and work 8cm/3¼in in rib as on back, ending with a 2nd row and inc one st in centre of last row. 40 sts.
Change to larger needles and cont in patt as foll:
1st row [P1, inc 1] 4 times, [K1, inc 1] twice, [P1, inc 1] 8 times, [K1, inc 1] twice, [P1, inc 1] 4 times. 60 sts.
2nd row MB, P3tog, K8, P6, K8, [MB, P3tog] twice, K8, P6, K8, MB P3tog.
3rd row P12, K6, P24, P12.
4th row P3tog, MB, K8, P6, K8, [P3tog, MB] twice, K8, P6, K8, P3tog, MB.
This sets position of patt. Cont as set, inc one st at each end of the next and every foll 5th row until there are 72 sts, then every foll 4th row until there are 102 sts. Cont

without shaping until sleeve measures 47cm/18½in from beg, ending with a WS row. Cast/bind off *loosely*.

COLLAR

With circular needle, cast on 114 sts. Work 28cm/11in in rounds of K1, P1 rib. Cast/bind off *loosely*.

FINISHING

Do not press.
Join shoulder seams. Sew in sleeves, with centre of sleeve to shoulder seam. Join side and sleeve seams. Sew cast on edge of collar to neck. Sew in shoulder pads.

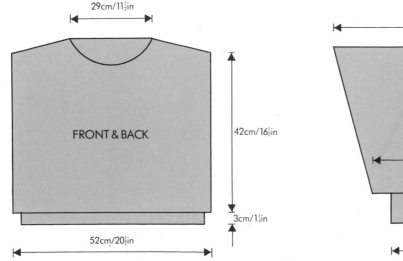

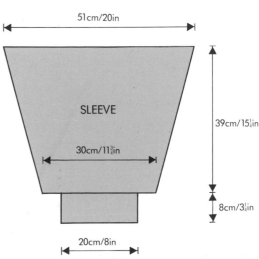

Calvin Klein

Calvin Klein's name is synonymous with assertive, urbane, yet wearable clothes. Ever since his launch in 1968 with three dresses and six coats, he has been recognized and successful. Bonwit Teller's, the leading New York store, placed a US $50,000 order for that first collection. Now Calvin Klein heads a multi-million dollar company, with clothing, furs, shoes, bags, bedlinen, menswear, make-up and scent bearing his name. He was the first designer to win the Coty Award in three consecutive years from 1973, and in 1975 was elected to the Coty Hall of Fame. He designs clothes with a soft, shimmering simplicity, using silks, cashmeres, mohairs and fine wools, often preferring neutral colours. 'I love clothes that are closely related to the body, and I hate unnecessary trimmings,' he says. 'The true luxury is simplicity', a view epitomized by the stunning silk two-piece featured here.

• MOCK TURTLENECK •

Calvin Klein's cardigan and mock turtleneck are the height of simple elegance. The original design is knitted in Joseph Galler's *Silk Tape Bamboo* (see page 123 for mail ordering). The tension quoted here also works using Anny Blatt's *Look Anny*, a synthetic substitute, which gives a firmer, shinier effect, not as luxurious, but reliable to knit.

(The turtleneck is sleeveless with matching rib edging.)

MATERIALS

8×50g/1¾oz of Joseph Galler's *Silk Tape Bamboo*
1 pair each of 3¾mm/US size 5 and 4mm/US size 6 knitting needles
2 buttons

SIZE

To fit 86-91cm/34-36in bust. See diagram for finished measurements.

TENSION/GAUGE

21 sts and 25 rows to 10cm/4in over st st on 4mm/US size 6 needles.

ABBREVIATIONS

See page 11.

BACK

With smaller needles, cast on 114 sts.
1st row (RS) K2, [P2, K2] to end.
2nd row P2, [K2, P2] to end.
Rep these last 2 rows 5 times more, then first row again.
Dec row [P3, P2tog] 22 times, P4. 92 sts.
Change to larger needles. Beg with a K row, cont in st st, dec one st at each end of every foll 4th row

twice, every foll 6th row 4 times, then foll alternate row once. 78 sts. Work 5 rows without shaping.

Shape sides

Next row (RS) K to end, inc one st at each end.
Cont inc at each end of every foll 5th row 7 times more. 94 sts. Cont without shaping until back measures 38cm/15in from beg, ending with a WS row.

Shape armholes

Cast/bind off 3 sts at beg of next 2 rows, then dec one st at each end of next row. 86 sts.
Cont without shaping until back measures 48cm/18¾in from beg, ending with a WS row.

Divide for opening

Next row (RS) K43 sts and leave on holder for right side of back neck, K1 into row below last st on st holder, K to end.
****Cont on these 44 sts until back measures 60cm/23½in from beg, ending with a WS row.

Shape neck and shoulder

Next row (RS) Cast/bind off 18 sts, K to end.
Leave these 26 sts on a spare needle for shoulder.
Rejoin yarn to neck edge of sts on holder for right side of neck.
Next row (WS) P1 into row below last st of first row of left side of neck, P to end. 44 sts.
Rep from ******, reversing all shaping.

FRONT

Work as given for back until front measures 55cm/21¾in from beg, ending with a WS row. 86 sts.

Shape neck

Next row (RS) K32 sts and leave on

holder for left side of neck, cast/bind off 22, K to end.
P one row on these 32 sts.
*****Cast/bind off 3 sts at beg of next row, 2 sts at beg of foll alternate row, then one st at beg of foll alternate row. 26 sts.
Work without shaping until front measures same as back to shoulders. Leave these 26 sts on a spare needle for shoulder.
Rejoin yarn to neck edge of sts on holder for left side of front. Rep from *******, reversing all shaping.

ARMHOLE BORDERS

Join shoulder seams. (See Note on page 109.)

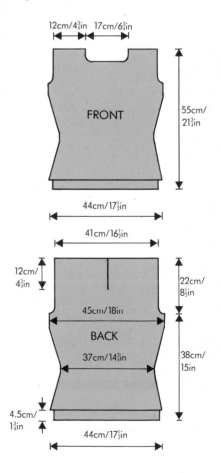

12cm/4¾in 17cm/6¾in

FRONT

55cm/21¾in

44cm/17½in

41cm/16½in

12cm/4¾in

22cm/8½in

45cm/18in

BACK

37cm/14¾in

38cm/15in

4.5cm/1¾in

44cm/17½in

With smaller needles and RS facing, pick up and K 118 sts evenly around armhole. Beg with a 2nd row, work 5 rows in rib as on back. Cast/bind off *loosely* in rib.

Note Shoulders should be grafted tog (see page 117). If you do not wish to graft, hold corresponding sets of sts for shoulders tog with K sides inside and cast/bind off a st from each needle tog.

NECKBAND

With smaller needles and RS facing, pick up and K 18sts up left back neck, 42 sts evenly around front neck and 18 sts down right back neck. 78 sts.
Beg with a 2nd row, work 3 rows in rib as on back.

Buttonhole row (RS) K2, yarn to front of work between needles, then to back of work over right hand needle and to front again between needles to make a new loop on right hand needle, P2tog, rib to end.
Cont in rib until neckband measures 6.5cm/2½in, ending with a WS row.
Next row (RS) As for first buttonhole row.
Cont in rib until neckband measures 7.5cm/3in from beg, ending with a 2nd row. Cast/bind off *loosely* in rib.

FINISHING

Press pieces lightly as instructed on yarn label, avoiding ribbing. Join side seams. Press seams. Sew on buttons.

·LONG-SLEEVED CARDIGAN·

MATERIALS

15×50g/1¾oz of Joseph Galler's *Silk Tape Bamboo*
1 pair each of 3¾mm/US size 5 and 5mm/US size 8 knitting needles
3¾mm/US size 5 circular needle 100cm/40in long
4 buttons

SIZE

To fit 86-91cm/34-36in bust. See diagram for finished measurements.

TENSION/GAUGE

19 sts and 23 rows to 10cm/4in over st st on 5mm/US size 8 needles.

ABBREVIATIONS

See page 11.

BACK

With smaller needles, cast on 102 sts.
1st row (RS) K2, [P2, K2] to end.
2nd row P2, [K2, P2] to end.
Rep these last 2 rows until rib measures 5cm/2in from beg, ending with a 2nd row and inc 4 sts evenly across the last row. 106 sts.
Change to larger needles. Beg with a K row, cont in st st until back measures 42cm/16½in from beg, ending with a WS row.

Shape armholes
Cast/bind off 3 sts at beg of next 2 rows. Dec one st at each end of next and foll 3 alternate rows. 92 sts.
Cont without shaping until back measures 66cm/26in from beg, ending with a WS row.

Shape shoulders and neck
Next row (RS) K28 sts and leave on a spare needle for right shoulder, cast/bind off 36 sts for back neck, K to end.
Leave these 28 sts on a spare needle for left shoulder.

RIGHT FRONT

With smaller needles, cast on 48 sts.
1st row (RS) [K2, P2] to end.
Rep last row until rib measures 5cm/2in from beg, ending with a WS row and inc 2 sts evenly across the last row. 50 sts.
Change to larger needles. Beg with a K row, cont in st st until front measures 37cm/14½in from beg, ending with a WS row.

Shape neck
Dec one st at beg of next and every foll 4th row 13 times in all, then

every foll 6th row twice more, AT
THE SAME TIME, when front
measures 42cm/16½in from beg,
ending with a RS row.

Shape armhole

Cast/bind off 3 sts at beg of next
row, then dec one st at end of foll
row and next 3 alternate rows.
Cont shaping neckline as given
until 28 sts rem.
Cont without shaping until front
measures 66cm/26in from beg,
ending with a WS row. Leave these
sts on a spare needle for right
shoulder.

LEFT FRONT

Work as given for right front,
reversing all shaping so that
neckline dec are worked at end of
RS rows instead of beg and
armhole shapings are worked at
beg of RS rows.

SLEEVES

With smaller needles, cast on 46 sts
and work 5cm/2in in rib as on
back, ending with a 2nd row and
inc 6 sts evenly across the last row.
52 sts.
Change to larger needles. Beg
with a K row, cont in st st, inc one st
at each end of 5th and every foll
6th row 16 times more. 86 sts.
P one row. Cont without shaping
until sleeve measures 52cm/20½in
from beg.

Shape top

Cast/bind off 5 sts at beg of next 12
rows. 26 sts. Cast/bind off *loosely*
knitwise.

FRONT BAND AND
NECKBAND

Join shoulder seams. (See Note
below.)
With circular needle and RS
facing, pick up and K 94 sts evenly
up right front, 71 sts up right side of
neck, 36 sts across back neck, 71
sts down left side of neck and 94 sts

down left side of front. 366 sts.
Beg with a 2nd row, work 3 rows in
rib as on back.

Buttonhole row Rib 6, P2tog, yarn
to back of work over right hand
needle to make a new loop on
right hand needle – called yarn
over needle or yon –, [rib 26,
P2tog, yon] 3 times, rib to end.
This completes 4 buttonholes. Cont
in rib until band measures 2.5cm/
1in from beg, ending with a 2nd
row.
Cast/bind off *loosely* in rib.

Note Shoulders should be grafted
tog. If you do not wish to graft, hold
corresponding sets of sts for
shoulders tog with K sides inside
and cast/bind off a st from each
needle tog. (For grafting, see page
117.)

FINISHING

Press pieces lightly as instructed
on yarn label, avoiding ribbing.
Sew in sleeves. Join side and
sleeve seams. Press seams. Sew on
buttons.

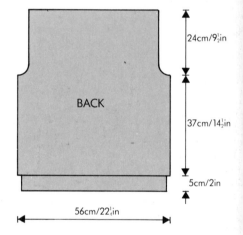

BACK
24cm/9½in
37cm/14½in
5cm/2in
56cm/22½in

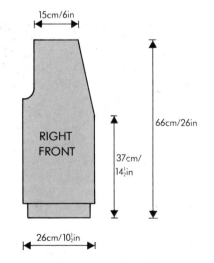

RIGHT FRONT
15cm/6in
66cm/26in
37cm/14½in
26cm/10½in

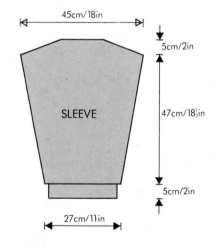

SLEEVE
45cm/18in
5cm/2in
47cm/18½in
5cm/2in
27cm/11in

Joan Vass

• *OOK HATS* •

Joan Vass's 'OOK' (One Of a Kind) hats are true originals; she mixes odd lengths of exclusive, beautiful yarns to create unique pieces. Any number of oddments in bouclé and double knitting novelty yarns can be used to emulate the examples shown here; strand several different colours together to achieve the correct bulky weight (UK double-knit, double-stranded).

Joan Vass herself does not believe in knitting to tension squares. Instead she prefers hand knitters to work to their own patterns and plans. Here at least, for the less experienced, details of the colour mixing and shaping of all the hat shapes is supplied to help get you started.

GREY BALACLAVA

MATERIALS

70g/2½oz of Woolgatherers' *Flaminia*
70g/2½oz of Woolgatherers' *Tartare (B)*
8mm/US size 11 circular needle 50cm/20in long
Set of four 8mm/US size 11 double pointed needles
8mm/US size K crochet hook

SIZE

To fit average women's size.

TENSION/GAUGE

10 sts and 16 rows over rib on 8mm/US size 11 needles

Note One strand of each of two types of yarn are used together throughout.

ABBREVIATIONS

dc – double crochet/US single crochet.
Also see page 11.

TO MAKE HAT

With circular needle, cast on 48 sts. Mark beg of the first round with a coloured thread, moving it up the hat as you work.
1st round [K2, P2] to end.
Rep this round 22 times more.
24th round K1, cast/bind off 16, rib to end.
Work 9 rows in rib on rem 32 sts.
34th round Casting on 16 sts over the 16 cast/bound off, rib to end. 48 sts.
Work 14 more rounds.

Shape top
Change to set of four double pointed needles.
Next round [Rib 14, K2tog] to end. 45 sts.
Next round [Rib 13, K2tog] to end. 42 sts.
Next round [Rib 12, K2tog] to end. 39 sts.
Next round [Rib 11, K2tog] to end. 36 sts.
Cont as set, dec sts on every round until shaping is complete.
Fasten off and secure ends tightly.

CROCHET DETAIL

With crochet hook, work 1 round in dc/sc along face opening. Fasten off. Make a crochet chain approximately 80cm/30in long and thread though lower edge of hat to tie at centre front.

SEA ANEMONE

MATERIALS

A total of 85g/3oz of Woolgatherers' *Flaminia* divided between 5 different colours
A total of 85g/3oz of Woolgatherers' *Tartare* divided between 5 different colours
8mm/US size 11 circular needle 50cm/20in long
Set of four 8mm/US size 11 double pointed needles
8mm/US size K crochet hook

SIZE

To fit average women's size

TENSION/GAUGE

10 sts and 16 rows to 10 cm square over rib on 8mm/US size 11 needles

Note One strand of two types of yarn is used together throughout.

ABBREVIATIONS

A – one strand of each yarn in first colour.
B – one strand of each yarn in second colour.
C – one strand of each yarn in third colour.
D – one strand of each yarn in fourth colour.
E – one strand of each yarn in fifth colour.
ch – chain; **tr** – treble crochet/US double crochet.
Also see page 11.

TO MAKE HAT

With circular needle and A, cast on
48 sts. Mark beg of the first round
with a coloured thread, moving it
up the hat as you work.
1st round: [K2, P2] to end.
Rep this round 4 times more. Cont
in rib as set, working in stripes of
14 rounds B, 6 rounds A, 4 rounds
C, 4 rounds D, 4 rounds E and 6
rounds A.
With B, P 5 rounds.

Shape top
Change to set of four double
pointed needles and cont in B
throughout.
Next round K to end.
Next round [K4, K2tog] to end.
40 sts.
Next round [K3, K2tog] to end.
32 sts.
Next round [K2, K2tog] to end.
24 sts.
Next round [K1, K2tog] to end.
16 sts.
Next round P to end.
Next round [K2tog] to end. 8 sts.
Next round [K2tog] to end. 4 sts.
Next round [K2tog] to end. 2 sts.
K2tog and fasten off.

CROCHET DETAIL

With crochet hook and A, into first
st of last of 5 purl rounds in B, work
1tr/dc, [make 9ch, then work 5tr/
dc into next st] to end, ending last
rep with 4tr/dc into same st as first
tr/dc. Fasten off.

BLUE BALACLAVA

MATERIALS

325g/11½oz of a variety of
lightweight and medium weight
yarns in various toning colours
1 pair of 10mm/US size 15 knitting
needles

10mm/US size 15 60cm/24in long
circular needle
1 cable needle
10mm/US size P crochet hook

SIZE

To fit average women's size.

TENSION/GAUGE

7½ sts and 12 rows to 10cm/4in
over moss stitch on 10mm/US size
15 needles.

Note 2, 3, 4 strands of any
combination of yarns can be used
together, but check tensions/
gauges of all variations carefully
before you begin this design.

ABBREVIATIONS

M1 – pick up loop lying between
sts and work into back of it.
m st – moss stitch/US seed stitch.
T2 – sl next st to cable needle to
front of work, K1, then K1 from
cable needle.
dc – double crochet/US single
crochet, sc.
Also see page 11.

FRONT

With pair of needles, cast on 6 sts.
1st row (RS) K1, sl next 2 sts to
cable needle to front of work, K2,
then K2 from cable needle, K1.
2nd row P3, M1, P3.
3rd row K1, T2, K1, T2, K1.
4th row P3, [K1, P1] into next st, P3.
5th row K1, T2, m st 2, T2, K1.
6th row P3, M1, m st 2, M1, P3.
7th row K1, T2, m st to last 3 sts, T2,
K1.
8th row P3, M1, m st to last 3 sts,
M1, P3.
Rep the last 2 rows until there are
44 sts.
Next row Patt 11, cast/bind off 22
sts, patt to end.

BACK

Next row Patt 11, cast on 22 sts,

patt 11. 44 sts.
Next row K1, T2, m st to last 3 sts,
T2, K1.
Next row P2, P2tog, m st to last 4
sts, P2tog, P2.
Cont as set to match front, dec one
st at either side of m st until 6 sts
rem. Cast/bind off.

HOOD

With circular needle and RS
facing, beg at right shoulder, pick
up and K 44 sts evenly around neck
opening.
Cont in rounds of K1, P1 rib until
hood measures 13cm/5in from beg.
Next round Rib 26, cast/bind off 14
sts, rib to end.
Cont in rounds on rem 30 sts until
hood measures 23cm/9in from beg.
Next round Rib to end, casting on
14 sts over the 14 cast/bound off.
44 sts.
Cont in rounds until hood
measures 26cm/10¼in from beg.

Shape top
Next round Rib 7, work 2 tog, rib
12, work 2 tog, rib 13, work 2 tog,
rib 6.
Cont to dec on every round as set,
until 8 sts rem, keeping all decs in
line.
Break off yarns, thread through
rem sts, pull up tight and fasten off.
With crochet hook and RS facing,
work one round in dc/sc along
lower edge (see page 119) and
around face opening. Fasten off.

CROCHET CONE TOP

MATERIALS

A total of 65g/2½oz of
Woolgatherers' *Flaminia* divided
between 7 different colours
A total of 65g/2½oz of
Woolgatherers' *Tartare (B)*
divided between 7 different colours

8mm/US size 11 circular needle
50cm/20in long
Set of four 8mm/US size 11 double
pointed needles
8mm/US size K crochet hook

SIZE

To fit average women's size.

TENSION/GAUGE

10 sts and 16 rows to 10cm over rib
on 8mm/US size 11 needles.

Note Two strands of yarn are used
together throughout.

ABBREVIATIONS

A – one strand each of *Flaminia*
and *Tartare (B)* in first colour.
B – one strand each of *Flaminia*
and *Tartare (B)* in second colour.
C – one strand each of *Flaminia*
and *Tartare (B)* in third colour.
D – one strand each of *Flaminia*
and *Tartare (B)* in fourth colour.
E – one strand each of *Flaminia*
and *Tartare (B)* in fifth colour.
F – one strand each of *Flaminia*
and *Tartare (B)* in sixth colour.
G – one strand each of *Flaminia*
and *Tartare (B)* in seventh colour.
ch – chain; **dc** – double crochet/US
single crochet.
Also see page 11.

TO MAKE HAT

With circular needle and A, cast on
48 sts. Mark beg of the first round
with a coloured thread, moving it
up the hat as you work.
1st round [K2, P2] to end.
Rep this round 6 times more. Cont
in rib as set working in stripes of 6
rounds B, 6 rounds C, 8 rounds B, 4
rounds D, 6 rounds E, 6 rounds F, 4
rounds G and 4 rounds B.
With A, P 5 rounds.

Shape top
Change to set of four double
pointed needles and cont in A
throughout.

Next round K to end.
Next round [K4, K2tog] to end.
40 sts.
Next round [K3, K2tog] to end.
32 sts.
Next round [K2, K2tog] to end.
24 sts.
Next round [K1, K2tog] to end.
16 sts.
Next round P to end.
Next round [K2tog] to end. 8 sts.
Next round [K2tog] to end. 4 sts.
Next round [K2tog] to end. 2 sts.
K2tog and fasten off.

CROCHET DETAIL

With crochet hook and B, into first
st of last purl round in A, work 1dc/
sc, work 1dc/sc into each st to end.
Next round [1dc/sc into next dc/sc,
miss/skip 1dc/sc] to end.
Cont as set until crochet measures
10cm/4in from beg, but change
colour to C after 5cm/2in. Work 3
loops of 9ch into last round,
fastening each loop with a dc/sc.
Fasten off.

HAT WITH PLAITS

MATERIALS

A total of 130g/5oz of
Woolgatherers' *Flaminia, Tartare
(B), Tartare* and *Shetland* divided
between 5 different colours
8mm/US size 11 circular needle
50cm/20in long
Set of four 8mm/US size 11 double
pointed needles
8mm/US size K crochet hook

SIZE

To fit average women's size

TENSION/GAUGE

10 sts and 16 rows to 10cm/4in
over rib on 8mm/US size 11
needles.

Note Either one strand of *Flaminia*
and *Tartare (B)* OR one strand of
Tartare and *Shetland* are used
together throughout.

ABBREVIATIONS

A – two strands of first colour.
B – two strands of second colour.
C – two strands of third colour.
D – two strands of fourth colour.
E – two strands of fifth colour.
dc – double crochet/US single
crochet. Also see page 11.

TO MAKE HAT

With circular needle and A, cast on
48 sts. Mark beg of the first round
with a coloured thread, moving it
up the hat as you work.
1st round [K2, P2] to end.
Rep this round 6 times more. Cont
in rib as set working in stripes of 6
rounds B, 6 rounds C, 8 rounds D, 5
rounds E, 5 rounds A, 6 rounds C
and 6 rounds D. With A, P 5 rounds.

Shape top
Change to set of four double
pointed needles and cont in A
throughout.
Next round K to end.
Next round [K4, K2tog] to end.
40 sts.
Next round [K3, K2tog] to end.
32 sts.
Next round [K2, K2tog] to end.
24 sts.
Next round [K1, K2tog] to end.
16 sts.
Next round P to end.
Next round [K2tog] to end. 8 sts.
Next round [K2tog] to end. 4 sts.
Next round [K2tog] to end. 2 sts.
K2tog and fasten off.

TOP DETAIL

Cut chosen yarn into 24 lengths of
25cm/10in and thread through top
of hat, securing each and plait.
Keeping plaits on inside of crochet,
work as foll: with crochet hook work
11dc/sc into top of crown. Work
6 rounds in dc/sc, then fasten off.

· KNITTING TECHNIQUE ·

USING ALTERNATIVE YARNS

Most patterns specify a yarn that has been tried and tested for the pattern given. However, it is possible to use substitutions, as long as you stick to the basic rule of knitting a tension or gauge sample first. Not only do yarns vary greatly in the way that they knit up (some heavier and thicker than others, or vice versa even though they look superficially similar) but different knitters work more tightly or more loosely – so that the needle size recommended in a commercial pattern or in this book may not suit you.

Aim to knit a square 10 cm by 10 cm (4 in by 4 in) as anything less than this is difficult to measure accurately. When you lay the sample out for measuring, do not cheat by pulling the work one way or the other to make it correspond to the dimensions in the instructions – this is counterproductive and will result in a badly fitting garment. Tension samples are normally given for a sample worked over stocking stitch, which is the easiest pattern for measuring over. Make sure that you start counting from a whole stitch, and do include even a half stitch for a correct answer.

If the work is too loose, the sample will be wider than the specified measurement. Change to a smaller needle – a half size will make all the difference – and then knit another sample.

If the work is too tight, the sample will be narrower than the specified measurement. Change to a larger size needle and knit another sample.

If the width is right, but the length slightly too much, then adjust the depth of the knitting as you work. If the shaping of armholes is crucial (as in set-in sleeve patterns) then the depth of the tension square is more important than the width – lose a stitch or two, depending on the pattern, on the width measurement. This rule for the depth also applies to a charted pattern, where the rows are strictly counted vertically. Too deep a stitch in the tension sample will affect the shaping of the motif overall.

To help you substitute yarns more easily, or to knit to the right tension, a number of yarn manufacturers give helpful advice on the ball band. Little diagrams specify the needle size normally used, give a sample tension square, and, most importantly, give you the yardage or meterage in the ball. Use this information to choose a yarn that knits to the same recommended needle size as specified in the pattern. Do not make the mistake of using a substitute yarn and buying only the same number of balls stated in the pattern for the original recommended yarn – make sure you are buying the same total *length* of yarn.

If at all possible, buy your yarns from a shop that is willing to put yarn to one side or at least give you an exchange system or credit note, especially when making a substitution with a yarn. As with any other craft, it is advisable to find a knowledgeable assistant who will check your purchases and give advice.

You can play safe by substituting only yarns of the same fibre content, for synthetics and wools knit up quite differently, even if you buy the same length of yarn in total. Many of the patterns featured in this book would also look just as attractive knitted in alternative yarns – say a double-knit cotton in place of a double-knit wool. Again, use the needle size as a clue to choosing a yarn of the right weight. The diagrams, giving dimensions of each pattern piece, will help you to work out how to use a completely different type of yarn, should you wish to be adventurous, and yet end up with the right-sized garment. Use them like a pattern, cutting out a tissue or newspaper shape to the dimensions given. Then you can lay your knitting on top of this, and knit freely until you achieve exactly the same proportions. Additional increases or decreases are then simply worked out at the edges of the garment, to adjust the fit.

Yarn types, tension/gauge, and needles

Yarn types, tension/gauge	Needle sizes US	Metric
Very fine weight, fine weight, or 2- or 3-ply Crochet cottons, baby yarns, dress-type yarns tension: 29-32 sts, 36-40 rows per 10cm/4in	3-4	2-4
Light weight, or 4-ply Sweaters, accessories, children's wear, summer yarns tension: 25-28 sts, 30-36 rows per 10cm/4in	3-6	3¼-4½
Medium weight, 4 ply, UK double-knit Cardigans, sweaters, men's wear, sports accessories tension: 21-24 sts, 24-30 rows per 10cm/4in	6-9	4-5½
Medium heavy weight, US heavy worsted Same uses as medium weight, bulkier tension: 17-20 sts, 20-26 rows per 10cm/4in	8-10	5-6
Bulky weight, double-stranded UK double-knit For jackets, outerwear, hats, novelties tension: 13-16 sts, 14-18 rows per 10cm/4in	10-11	6-8
Extra bulky, novelties, fur-type, bouclés Same uses as bulky weight tension: 9-12 sts, 10-14 rows per 10cm/4in	11-15	8-10

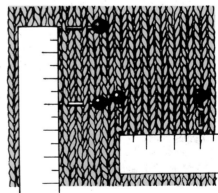

·TECHNICAL SECTION·

FINISHING TECHNIQUES

Blocking

Blocking makes a great difference to the finished effect of a piece of knitting, and is well worth the extra time needed to do it properly. Slamming a steam iron on to a freshly finished piece of work and backstitching it together to wear that night is often tempting, but usually regretted.

Use a folded blanket or pad of felt, covered with an old sheet. Pin out the garment sections to the dimensions given in the diagrams for your own size (a). Use pins at frequent intervals – about every 1cm (½in).

For yarns that cannot be steamed or ironed (the label for the yarn will give instructions in many cases) simply lay a damp or dry cloth on top of the pinned-out shape and leave it overnight for the knitting to settle into shape.

Hold a steam iron just above the knitting, then press down lightly, not weighting the knitting, to let the vapour do the job (b). Do not iron backwards or forwards. With ribbed or raised patterns, you may need to fluff up the knitting while it is still warm, even lifting it off the pins to do so. Pat back

and re-pin. Do not press welts as this reduces their elasticity.

As a rule, wool can be pressed with a warm iron over a damp cloth; synthetics require a cool iron and a dry cloth; cotton and silks, a hot iron and a wet cloth; similarly for mohair, but fluff it up as you press. Metallic yarns cannot generally be ironed as they may melt or at least tarnish.

Finishing

There are three main ways to make a seam in knitting, each one with its own uses, but many knitters find that one or other of these methods suits them best. For example, many skilled knitters prefer to use the invisible method, even around armholes, as it produces a fine, flat seam. Backstitch gives a tough seam and is recommended where the seam is being made across the direction of the knitting, as in curved shoulder seams. An edge-to-edge seam is made very quickly and is probably the most popular way.

Backstitch Mark off the area to be joined equally, counting the stitches evenly and pinning the two edges, right sides together. Secure the thread with two running stitches, then push the needle through from front to back, and then to the front again, the distance of one stitch. Reinsert the needle at the beginning of the first stitch, and bring it up to the front one stitch-space further along to the left. Continue in this way until the seam is finished. To keep the work regular, pull your needle out of the knitting and ease the following thread through gently on each stitch.

Edge-to-edge Prepare the edges to be joined as for the backstitch seam, pinning evenly. Start with two running stitches, then pass the needle from back to front through two parallel stitches, on each edge. Work back into the next stitch along to the left, pushing the needle from front to back this time. Continue zig-zag fashion along the seam, making sure that the stitches on each piece of knitting to be joined are perfectly lined up.

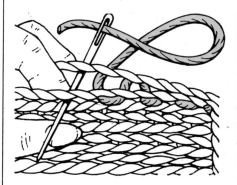

Invisible seam This seam is best applied to knitting that has been worked to the edge of every row, without each first stitch being slipped for a tight effect. There is no need to pin the seam first, just hold up the two edges as shown, right sides facing up. Pick up a horizontal bar, either inside the first stitch, or between the first and second stitch at the edge of the work, and repeat on the second edge. Pull the thread enough to draw the edges together, but not so tightly that the length of the seam puckers. This seam is very good for matching ribbed welts, for example when they are striped, or for making smooth side seams in stocking stitch knitting.

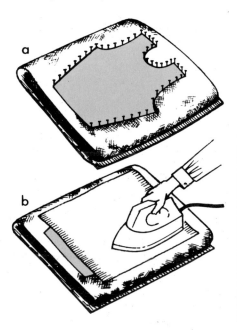

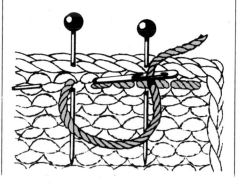

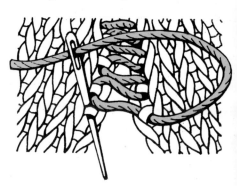

Grafting

Grafting is not strictly a seam, but a method of joining two looped edges of knitting. It can also be used when something is unpicked and lengthened or shortened, above a welt for example. It also makes a fine shoulder seam in stocking stitch work if you leave the stitches on a pin and place them together for joining, as shown.

One method (a) holds both edges on parallel needles: insert the threaded needle purlwise into the first stitch, then knitwise through the first stitch on the needle behind, then knitwise through the *first* stitch on the front needle again. Slip these two stitches off. Pass the needle purlwise through the second stitch on the front needle, purlwise through the second stitch on the back needle, knitwise through the same second stitch on the front needle again, and slip off. Continue along the row.

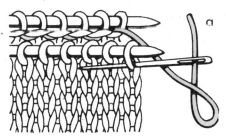

A second method (b) is to slip both raw edges off the knitting needles, press lightly to flatten and hold the edges, then literally 'weave' a threaded darning needle through the stitches, as shown.

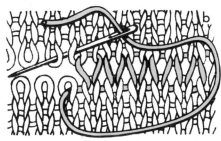

For all sewing methods, use a blunt-ended darning needle with a large eye for easy threading. A blunt tip slips easily between the stitches, without splitting the yarn. For knitted pieces thicker than 4-ply (worsted), use a matching 3- or 4-ply wool for making seams.

USING COLOURS

Joining colours at the beginning of a row

The simplest way to join in a colour is to tie the ends together at the beginning of the row. Leave a sufficient length to undo the knot and darn both ends into the edge of the knitting before making seams.

Splicing

An alternative method is to splice the ends of the yarn. Use this when joining two lengths of the same colour, when yarn is scarce or very expensive. Unravel the ends of both the old and new yarns for about 2-3 cm/1 in and twist these round each other. Rolling the spliced ends between moistened finger and thumb helps to bind them. Knit over the re-made yarn carefully to ensure that the threads do not slip apart.

Adding a new colour at the beginning of a row

A different colour can be added at the beginning of a row by wrapping the previous and the new colour yarns together and knitting or purling two or three stitches with both (a). Leave the first colour (with sufficient end at the back to be darned in after) and

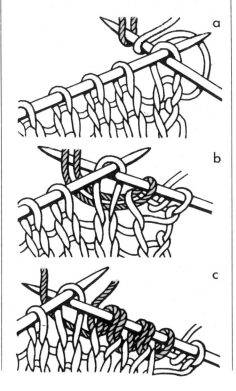

continue with the new colour strand only (b). On the next row knit or purl the doubled stitches as single ones (c).

Adding colour in the middle of a row

The same method is used for introducing a new colour strand into the middle of a piece of knitting. Either splice the ends, as above, or double the strands for a few stitches. The first colour can be stranded or woven across the back of the knitting if that colour is to be picked up again in the same row. Be careful not to pull the thread too tightly across the back when reintroducing it further along.

Stranding and weaving colours

There are two ways of working more than one colour into knitting along each row. If the pattern repeats over not more than six stitches it is possible to let the second or subsequent colour strands lie flat across the back of the knitting, merely twisting them round the yarn being worked before reintroducing them into the knitting. Contrast yarns are joined at the beginning of the row, then looped loosely across the back of the work on knit rows or across the front on purl rows. This method is impractical where small blocks of one colour are used at a distance from each other as the strands will catch on jewellery or buttons when the finished garment is in use.

For regular but more distant pattern repeats the different coloured yarns are woven in as the knitting progresses, as shown below.

A third and extremely practical alternative when working in patches of colour, for example, a multi-coloured single motif, is to wind small bobbins of the various yarns around yarn holders manufactured for the purpose or on to small spools of card or plastic or simply into small handmade balls. This is often called block knitting.

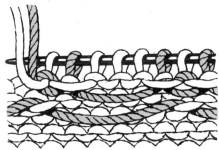

Stranding Join in the various colours at the beginning of the row. Carry the second or subsequent colours loosely across the back of the work until needed. The frequency of use of the various colours holds the stitches in place without holes appearing. (This is the traditional Fairisle method.) On purl rows the pattern is read in reverse from the chart, from left to right. The contrast colours are left loosely stranded across the front of the work.

Weaving in colour Knit the first stitch (a) in the main colour, but loop the contrast yarn across it before wrapping the yarn around the needle.

Make the second stitch (b) in the contrast colour (according to the colour chart) laying the first colour over the top of the yarn in the same way as before, while forming the stitch. Continue overlaying the alternative colours in this way, maintaining an even tension.

Purl rows (c) are worked in the same manner with the various strands twisted at the front of the work.

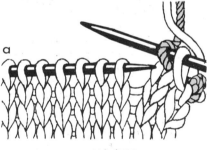

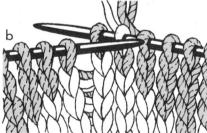

Block knitting Where colours are used in small areas it is easier to wind small balls of the various yarns used, even if the same motif occurs in the same row of knitting again. If the gap is over twenty stitches between colourwork, block knitting is easier to manage and prevents long threads pulling across the back of the knitting. You may work several clusters of little balls at intervals across the knitting. This looks complicated at first but soon becomes quicker to handle. The only important technique to remember is that the coloured yarn must be crossed over the next one used, otherwise holes will appear around the edge of the motif. The technique shown works equally well on motifs that run vertically as well as horizontally through a pattern.

When changing colour on a knit row (a) ensure that the yarn colour being dropped is looped across the top of the yarn being introduced. On the following purl row the yarns will twine together.

On a purl row (b) ensure that the yarn being dropped is looped across the top of the yarn being introduced. On the following knit row the yarns will twine together.

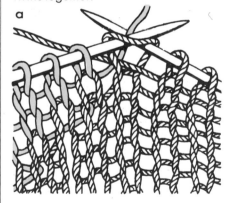

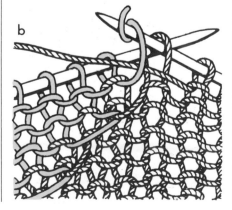

Swiss darning

This is a method of reinforcing or covering the surface of stocking stitch with another colour. The result looks exactly like a stocking stitch finish. It is important to use the same weight of yarn for the embroidery as for the knitting itself, otherwise the stitches will not be covered neatly.

This stitch is also a good method for thickening up a small motif area if you find that a yarn substitute has worked out a little thinner than you anticipated in comparison with the surrounding knitted areas.

Swiss darning is also an alternative method if you find weaving or stranding yarns for motifs difficult to do: any pattern that is graphed or charted for stocking stitch work can be Swiss darned instead, but it is advisable to do so for small areas only, as the knitting is obviously thickened up by the embroidery and would be unsuitable over large areas.

Secure the embroidery thread behind the work with two running stitches and bring the needle out at the front to the bottom of the first stitch to be covered. Take the needle up to the top of the same stitch and pass it under the base loops of the stitch above. Now return the needle to the first point of entry and push it under the two loops of the stitch below (a). This first stitch will now be completely covered, and the needle is in position to work up to the top of the next stitch to the left.

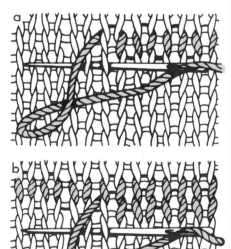

To work the second row (b), fasten off the thread and begin again at the right with the right side of the knitting facing you. Alternatively, turn the whole piece of knitting upside down and work back across the surface in the same way. Bring out the needle in the middle of the last stitch worked on the first row, and pick up two loops of the stitch lying directly below.

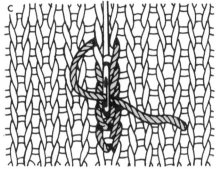

To work Swiss darning vertically (c), the first stitch is covered as described above but the needle is then taken under the top of the stitch below. Push the needle up to the front in the centre of the stitch above, anchoring it under the horizontal bar each time.

CROCHET FOR KNITTERS

Crochet for the whole of a garment goes in and out of fashion – but crochet for details on knitted sweaters or cardigans is a useful addition to any knitter's technique. A simple, plain shape can be enlivened by adding a crocheted edge to a collar, or to the button band. Add a little luxury to a garment knitted in an economical wool or cotton by using an expensive yarn, mohair, angora, or glittery thread, for a picot or other edge.

Crochet work is also useful for reinforcing or neatening cast-on edges. The method described below gives strength on a welt without affecting elasticity. Alternative decorative edges are shown.

Basic chain To start a basic crochet chain make a slip loop around the end of the crochet hook. Loop the yarn around the crochet needle behind the slip loop (a).

Pull the yarn through the slip loop so that only one loop remains on the needle (b). Continue forming the chain, holding the yarn behind it.

Double crochet/single crochet A double crochet/single crochet stitch is made by inserting the hook into the last but one stitch of the base or foundation chain (a). (On a knitted edge make two chains and then insert the hook into the next stitch on the edge.)

Loop the yarn around the hook, and pull the loop through the chain, but not through the loop already on the hook. (b). There are now two loops on the hook.

Now make a loop over the hook with the yarn. Pull this through the two loops on the hook in one go (c). Only one chain remains on the needle.

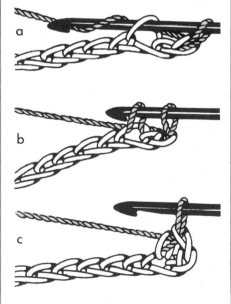

Treble crochet/double crochet A treble crochet/double crochet stitch is longer. At the beginning of every row or when starting on a knit edge, make a chain of three stitches to bring the hook up to the right height (a).

Wrap the yarn around the hook *before* inserting it into the next stitch, and pull a loop through (to make three loops on the hook), (b).

Wind the yarn around the hook and draw this loop through two of the loops on the hook (c).

Wind the yarn around the hook again, and draw this through the two remaining loops on the hook, to leave only one loop (d).

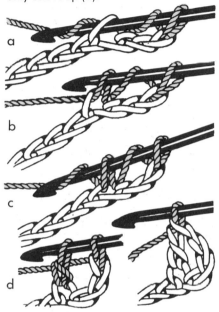

Edgings in crochet
For a firm edge over casting on, work one row or two of the double crochet (single crochet) over the cast-on row (a). This is particularly useful on edges without ribbed or garter stitch welts, to prevent curling.

A picot edge is made by securing the yarn to the right-hand corner of the edge; make a chain in the first stitch, then * make three chains, then one double crochet/single crochet into the first chain, miss one stitch, make one single chain into the next stitch, * and repeat these steps along the whole edge (b).

For a loop edging, make a series of chains (the number will depend on the thickness of the yarn and the size of the loop you prefer) anchoring the chain at regular intervals along the edge of the knitting with a double crochet/ single crochet stitch (c).

For a firmer effect, for example with a fine crochet cotton or silk, make double crochet/single crochet stitches over the base row of loops, to give them a neat ribbed look (d).

Shell edging can be made to any size depending on the number and length of the treble stitches/double used. A small edging for fine work is made by forming one chain, then two trebles/doubles into the same stitch, one chain again, then skip one stitch on the knit edge, and repeat all along the row (e).

Very large shells can be made using as many as six trebles/doubles into every third or fourth stitch on an edge (f).

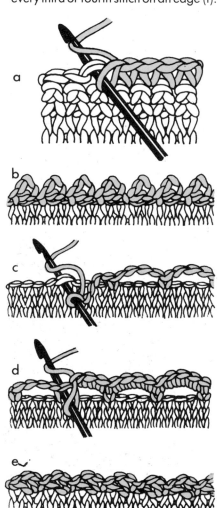

Instructions for the Joan Vass crocheted sweater, *Baby Iguana*, on page 102 are given in the pattern instructions, using the stitches illustrated here.

DESIGNING CHARTS

A number of the patterns in this book give you basic shapes which could be re-used if you want to make up your own motifs on the front, back or sleeves. The Vittadini sweaters with bold, floral designs (see pages 38-9) are beautiful examples of well-planned designs; the motifs vary on each sleeve, and the backs are unified with the fronts by taking the decoration over one side of the shoulder. In the Hympendahl design (see page 84) the motif area is related to the main part of the sweater by mixing the yarns, so that the motif does not stick out too sharply from the shape. In Sasha Kagan's *Squiggle* sweater (see page 28) the design appears to use many colours, but was conceived so that no more than two strands are used in any one row, for speedier knitting.

Lainey's *Marcus* sweater (see page 60) has a strong, painterly quality, with areas of colour 'splashed' on to the surface of the knit to contrast with the subdued colours of the textured wools.

All these designs give you suggestions of how: a) balance in an idea; b) clever use of colouring; and c) unusual mixes of yarn materials should be thought out carefully whenever you plan a charted design.

The first step is to knit a tension square in the yarn you will be using. Measure the work carefully, so that you have an exact dimension for the stitch size. Now draw up a sheet of graph paper to the size of the stitches you will be using. (Double the measurements if the stitches are fine, otherwise the grid will be impossible to draw or read.) This is a much more realistic and accurate method than using commercially bought graph paper, where the squares do not correspond to the shape of your knitting, and will give you an unfinished impression of the completed design. Because there are more rows than stitches to a square of knitting, a motif will work out longer than a chart planned on regular squared paper. (Knitting chart paper is available in some specialist stores.)

If you are using a picture from a magazine, and wish to use it same size, then trace round the outline using carbon paper, straight on to the prepared grid (a).

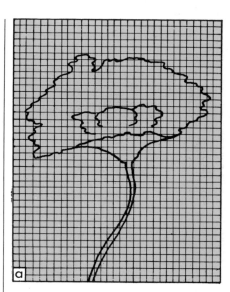

Formalize the outline by colouring in the shape to conform to the stitch squares (b). True curves are impossible to achieve in knitting.

Shade in with colours or with colour symbols, the various areas you will use in the knitting, and give a key if necessary (c).

For speed of reading, mark all the rows that will be worked in knit on the right-hand side of the chart, with uneven numbers, starting at 1. Rows to be knitted in purl stitch and worked on the wrong side, should be marked on the left-hand side of the chart, with even numbers starting at 2 (d).

If you want to use a design that is bigger or smaller than the area of your

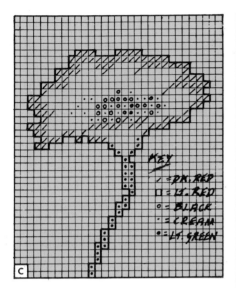

KEY

/ = DK. RED
□ = LT. RED
o = BLACK
· = CREAM
● = LT. GREEN

c

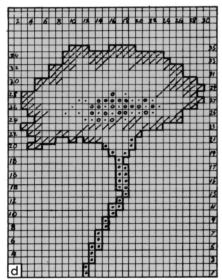

2 4 6 8 10 12 14 16 18 20 22 24 26 28 30

d

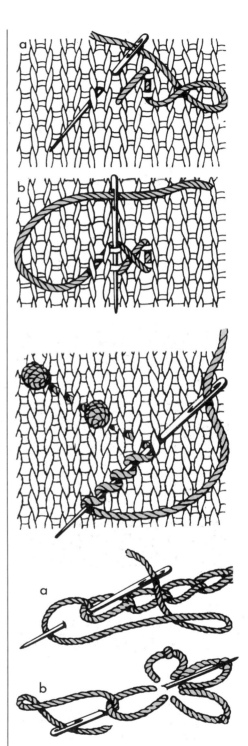

SIMPLE EMBROIDERY STITCHES

Cross stitch Secure the yarn and bring to the front on the right-hand side of the area to be covered. Bring the darning needle through to the left at the base of the first stitch. Take the needle and thread diagonally to the top and to the right of the stitch, insert the needle, and bring the needle point out directly below, on a level with the first exit point of the thread (a).

Cross the yarn over the top of the first diagonal. Push the needle through to the back, to the left of the stitch being decorated, keeping the needle tip on a level with the top of the first diagonal. Bring the needle tip out to the front again, one stitch along to the left, at the bottom of the line and to the left of the next stitch to be decorated. Repeat all these steps across the knitting (b).

A better effect is achieved working across the row stitch by stitch, rather than making a line of diagonals and working back across them to the right on the return row, but you might prefer this method if you are short of time.

French knots Secure the thread behind the knitting in the usual way. Bring the thread through to the right side of the work, looped under the stitch where the knot is to be made. Keeping the darning needle in the knitting as shown, wind the thread that comes out of the knitting around the tip four times, then pull the needle through gently. Use your thumbnail to arrange the 'spiral' of the knot neatly, then push the needle tip through to the back of the work in the same spot. Carry the embroidery thread loosely across the back of the knitting to the next spot for a knot to be made.

Chain stitch Secure the thread and bring it out to the right side of the work. Using the thumbnail of the left hand, secure a loop of thread on the surface of the knitting while you catch up a small stitch in the knitted fabric. Pull the thread through. Reinsert the needle in the same spot where the first thread came out, and form a second loop with the thread, holding it down in the same manner.

sweater, you will have to scale up or reduce the design. Draw over the surface of the picture (use tracing paper if you don't want to spoil it) dividing the motif into squares of equal size. It does not matter if they are 1cm/ ½in or 10cm/4in, as long as they are regular.

On a separate sheet of paper, draw up a block of squares approximating to the area you want for the finished design. Follow the original picture, and copy the outline of it on to this second grid, keeping the shape the same within each square so that you do not lose the proportions. Make any adjustments freehand, then trace the design on to your knitting chart as described above.

When embroidering a line on knitting, it is helpful to tack it flat first, because the knitting stretches out of shape as you hold it in your hands to embroider.

BUTTONS, BANDS AND EDGES

Buttonholes

Finishing touches such as well-made buttonholes or well-applied button bands make all the difference to your knitting and prolong the life of the garment. There are many ways to make buttonholes – most patterns give instructions within their details – but these two give a good effect.

Vertical buttonholes Knit to the base where the buttonhole is to be made. Split the work in two, holding one half on a stitch-holder. Turn the knitting and continue in pattern up the first side of the buttonhole to the required depth (a). Leave the yarn hanging at the end of the last row.

　　Join in a new ball of knitting at the base of the buttonhole, return the held stitches to the needle and knit in pattern up the second half of buttonhole to the level of the first half worked, *minus* one row; this last will be made in the original yarn. Using a darning needle, weave in the loose starting and finishing ends of the yarn used for the second half of the buttonhole (b). Continue across the whole button band in the original yarn until the position of the next buttonhole is reached. Repeat these two stages.

Horizontal buttonholes (a) Use the one-row method. Knit to the base of the first buttonhole, then bring the yarn forward to the front of the work. Slip the first stitch on to the right-hand needle, take the yarn to the back of the needle, and cast off one stitch without knitting, by slipping the second stitch, and passing the first slipped stitch back over it. Repeat this process for the required length of the buttonhole.

　　(b) Slip the last stitch back on to the left-hand needle and turn the work round. Place the yarn behind the needles. Cast on the same number of stitches as just cast off, to replace them plus one extra stitch. Before placing this last stitch on the left-hand needle, take the yarn to the front of the work once more. Turn work, slip the first stitch from the left-hand to the right-hand needle, then pass the extra cast-on stitch over it and off the needle, to close the buttonhole neatly.

　　(c) Knit in pattern across the rest of the row, and make subsequent buttonholes in the same way.

Button bands

Button bands should be knitted slightly shorter than the length of the front edge to which they will be attached. It is best to knit both the button band and the buttonhole band on the same needles, side by side, using two balls of wool so that the tension on both has more chance of being equal. You can also use safety pins or coloured thread to mark the button position on the same row as the buttonhole, so that the bands can be mounted exactly on a parallel. This device helps to prevent over-stretching or uneven stretching.

　　To attach a button band smoothly, count up the front edge of the knitting, placing pins every six rows or so (a). Place the button band alongside these pins, also counting the number of rows equally between the markers.

　　Oversew the button band as neatly as possible from the *right* side (b). Working on the wrong side gives a lumpy ridge down the front of the work.

　　Collars are stitched to necklines in the same way, counting and pinning regularly on the neck edge first, and counting an even number of stitches on the collar piece to place between each section of the neck edge (c). The number of stitches will only be even, *not equal*, as the collar knitting will probably run at right angles to the knitted body of the garment.

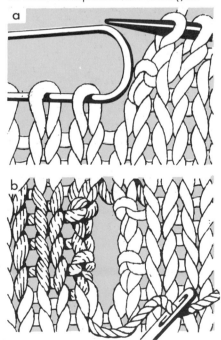

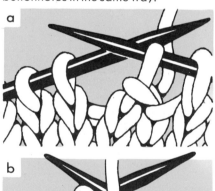

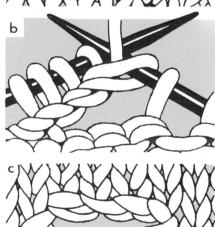

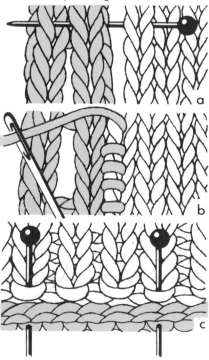

· *Yarn Suppliers* ·

UK (for all yarns mentioned in text by trade name see also Mail Order form next page)

Argyll Wools
Priestley Mills (no USA or Australian distribution)
Pudsey
W. Yorks LS28 9LT

Laines Anny Blatt
Bull Bridge
Ambergate
Derby DE5 2EY

DMC
Dunlicraft Ltd
Pullman Road
Wigston
Leicester LE8 2DY
(Mail Order form see next page)

Joseph Galler Yarns
(Mail Order form see next page)

Hayfield
Hayfield Textiles
Glusburn
Keighley
W. Yorks BD20 8QP

Pingouin Yarns
French Wools Ltd
7-11 Lexington Street
London W1R 4BU

Rowan Yarns
Green Lane Mill
Washpit
Holmfirth
Huddersfield
W. Yorks HD7 1RW

Scheepjeswol
PO Box 48
Unit 7 Colemeadow Road
North Moons Moat
Redditch
Worcs B98 9N2

Sirdar
Flanshaw Lane
Alverthorpe
Wakefield
W. Yorks WF2 9ND

Twilley's
H.G. Twilley
Roman Mill
Stamford
Lincs PE9 1BG

AUSTRALIA

Laines Anny Blatt
Anny Blatt AUST Pty Ltd
26 Punch Street
Artarmon
NSW 2064

DMC
Olivier AUST Pty Ltd
47-57 Collins Street
Alexandria
NSW 2015

Joseph Galler Yarns
(Mail Order Form see next page)

Hayfield
Panda Yarns (International) Pty Ltd
17-27 Brunswick Road
East Brunswick
VIC 3057

Pingouin Yarns
Pingouin AUST Pty Ltd
47-57 Collins Street
Alexandria
NSW 2015

Rowan Yarns
Sunspun Enterprises Ltd
195 Canterbury Road
CA 3126

Scheepjeswol
Thorobred Scheepjeswol
64 Balmain Street
Richmond
VIC 3121

Sirdar
Coats Patons AUST Pty Ltd
PO Box 110
321-355 Ferntree Gully Road
Mount Waverley
VIC 3149

Twilley's
Panda Yarns (address above)

USA

Laines Anny Blatt
24770 Crestview Court
Farmington
MI 48018

DMC Yarns
107 Trumbull Street
Elizabeth
NJ 07206

Joseph Galler Yarns
27 West 20th Street
New York
NY 10011

Hayfield
c/o Shepherd Wools Inc
711 Johnson Avenue
Blaine
Washington 98230

Pingouin Wools
Pingouin Box 100
Highway 45
Jamestown
SC 29453

Rowan Yarns
Westminster Trading
5 Northern Boulevard
Amhurst
NH 03031

Scheepjeswol, Inc
155 Lafayette Avenue
N. White Plains
NY 10603

Sirdar
Kendex Corporation
31332 Via Colinas 107
Westlake Village
CA 91362

Twilley's
c/o Rainbow Gallery
13615 Victory Boulevard
Suite 245
Van Neys
CA 91401

Acknowledgments

First I should like to thank Peggy and Kevin Kelly without whose generous hospitality in New York, this book would never have been written.

To all the designers who so willingly agreed to cooperate with me, supplied pattern instructions, graphs and charts, and to those also who very kindly lent valuable garments for many months while the book was in preparation, I express my gratitude.

A major contribution to this book was made by Elizabeth Jones, and her assistant, Joanna Hurn, of Woolgatherers, Chiswick, who provided expert pattern checkers, suitable yarns, and agreed to supply several of the more exclusive designs by mail order to anyone, anywhere, so that no reader would be disadvantaged by living far from a main yarn centre. I am also very grateful to Mary Harvey and Sabine Schweinsberg for their assistance with the European research.

Special acknowledgment is due to Sue Roberts, who created most of the hand-knitting instructions and worked out many charts with great efficiency in a remarkably short space of time. Thanks are also due to Sally Harding who supplied expert help and advice for the American edition. June Mackintosh devised the patterns for the Calvin Klein and the Perry Ellis designs, including the chart for the latter which was a considerable task done beautifully. Jill Carrott provided the pattern and the hand-knitted sample for the Beatrice Hympendahl sweater, and Eva Yates the same for the Bill Gibb sweater — my thanks to both of them for meticulous work.

Thanks are also expressed to The Scotch House, Knightsbridge, London for supplying skirts, trousers and the mohair scarves; to Perry Ellis, Calvin Klein, and Adrienne Vittadini in New York who lent me their own accessories; to the Joan Vass shop in London for the loan of a skirt and earrings to match the Baby Iguana sweater; to Butler and Wilson for the earrings to match the Bill Gibb sweater; and to Bill Gibb himself for the gold lace to decorate his own design, and for his encouragement, which was most appreciated.

The following designers can supply a limited number of yarn kits to match their patterns; please write for further details to:

Sandy Black
Tanner Place
54-58 Tanner Street
London SE1 3PH

Sasha Kagan
(Exclusively Yours)
12 Great Oak Street
Llanidloes, Powys
Wales SY18 6BU

Woolgatherers Order form

10 Devonshire Road, London W4   Tel: 995 6813

STYLE		SIZE	PRICE £	PRICE $	QUANTITY	AMOUNT ENCLOSED
Vicky Mora	*ZigZag**	ONE SIZE	89.50	120.00		
Beatrice Hympendahl	*Sweater*	ONE SIZE	36.50	52.00		
Joan Vass	*Dog Tooth Stripes*	34"	46.50	65.00		
		36"	48.50	73.00		
		38"	52.50	79.00		
Joan Vass	*Baby Iguana*	34"	47.50	67.00		
		36"	49.50	75.00		
		38"	54.50	80.00		
Joan Vass	*'Ook' Hats*					
	Sea Anemone Col-1		9.95	20.00		
	Sea Anemone Col-2		9.95	20.00		
	Crochet Cone Top		9.95	20.00		
	Hat with Plaits		9.95	20.00		
	Grey Balaclava		9.95	20.00		
	Blue Balaclava		14.95	20.00		
Louis Dell'Olio	*Aran**	ONE SIZE	18.50	30.00		
Calvin Klein *Cardigan* + 'Shell'	*Look Anny** *Silk Tape*		73.50 265.00	SEE US STOCKISTS' LISTS		
Perry Ellis	*Dragon Cardigan*	34" 36"	59.50	82.00		

Please complete this form in **Clear Block Letters** — marking the size required with a tick in the space provided.

Prices include postage and packing but not US Customs or State Taxes.

NAME_____

ADDRESS_____

_____

POSTCODE_____ TELEPHONE_____

I enclose cheque/PO for £_____

 " " /Money Order for $_____
or debit my Access/Barclaycard/Mastercard/American Express

Account Number_____

Signed_____

--------------------------------✂--------------------------------

CUT AND DETACH TO KEEP

HOW TO ORDER. Please fill in the Order Form above and send it with your cheque made payable to **WOOLGATHERERS** to the address on the Order Form. All prices include VAT at 15%. Kits should reach you within 21 days from our receipt of your order. If for any reason there is likely to be a delay, we will give you the option of cancelling, or choosing another style or colour.

*COLOURS & SIZING. Most of the knitwear is offered in one colourway only. We do, however, stock other colours of most yarns so if you would like to make up your own colours we will be happy to send you shade cards of the yarn(s) concerned if you write to us enclosing 40p per card plus s.a.e. Sizing is inevitably affected by personal preferences.

GUARANTEE. We hope that you will like the kit which you have bought from us and will enjoy knitting and/or wearing it! If for any reasons, however, you do not, and you return it to us undamaged and unused within 14 days, we will refund your money without question together with the cost of your postage in returning it to us.

CARE INSTRUCTIONS. All our knitwear should be washed carefully by hand using Woolite or a similar specialist detergent and dried flat out of the sun. We recommend that in hard water areas some fabric softener should be used.